"Carlene and Carolyn DeRoo offer a refreshing and p........ spective journey toward personal understanding that provides the opportunity for self-reflection. This book provides the tools and mechanisms for understanding in ourselves the influence of family, society, and culture on one's self acceptance and self growth! This book is a must-read for all who seek to know "what's right with me."

> —Thomas W. Miller, Ph.D., ABPP, is professor of Health Promotion Science and Allied Health at the University of Connecticut, a Fulbright Senior Scholar in Psychology, author of several books and publications, a diplomate of the American Board of Professional Psychology in Clinical Psychology and fellow of the American Psychological Association, Association of Psychological Science, and the Royal Society of Medicine

"What's Right with Me is the perfect vehicle for positive change and personal growth. Authors Carlene and Carolyn DeRoo take the reader on a step-by-step journey of self-exploration and rediscovery of personal strength. Their program of change is based on psychological science, and the exercises in each chapter help the reader achieve a new way of thinking. This book is a wonderful product of the new positive psychology movement and an excellent self-help tool."

> —Donna Wollerman Ronan, Ph.D., licensed clinical psychologist in private practice and director of the Psychological Training and Consultation Center of Central Michigan University's allied health clinics

"What's Right with Me is an excellent, health-oriented book which serves nicely as both a text and a workbook. It holds forth a practical healing perspective which releases the reader from needless restrictions in thinking and challenges detrimental mindsets. It encourages honesty without fear and confronts preconceptions about ourselves which hold us back. By highlighting a realistic life balance, readers have the opportunity to reconfigure positive parts of themselves which have been neglected or hidden and also reclaim aspects of themselves which may have been suppressed or forgotten. The book facilitates a fair and balanced view of ourselves, inviting us to experience a new aliveness through a more accurate appreciation of our true healthy selves. The tone rejoices in exploration and flows with themes of generosity and love as we learn to be kinder and gentler toward ourselves. Its foundation is solidly intellectual yet accessible to a broad audience—a great book for any person to work through."

> —Jeremy P. Crosby, Ph.D., clinical psychologist with the Specialized PTSD Treatment Program at Robert J. Dole VA Medical and Regional Office Center in Wichita, KS

what's right with me

positive ways to celebrate your strengths, build self-esteem & reach your potential

CARLENE DEROO, PH.D.
CAROLYN DEROO

New Harbinger Publications, Inc.

Publisher's Note

This publication is designed to provide accurate and authoritative information in regard to the subject matter covered. It is sold with the understanding that the publisher is not engaged in rendering psychological, financial, legal, or other professional services. If expert assistance or counseling is needed, the services of a competent professional should be sought.
Distributed in Canada by Raincoast Books.

Copyright © 2006 by Carolyn DeRoo and Carlene DeRoo
New Harbinger Publications, Inc.
5674 Shattuck Avenue
Oakland, CA 94609
www.newharbinger.com

Cover and text design by Amy Shoup; Cover image by Todd Pearson/Photodisc/Getty Images;
Acquired by Tesilya Hanauer;
Edited by Carole Honeychurch

Library of Congress Cataloging-in-Publication Data

DeRoo, Carlene.
  What's right with me : positive ways to celebrate your strengths, build self-esteem, and reach your potential / Carlene DeRoo and Carolyn DeRoo.
      p. cm.
  Includes bibliographical references.
  ISBN 1-57224-442-9
  1. Positive psychology. 2. Self-esteem. 3. Self-actualization (Psychology) I. DeRoo, Carolyn. II. Title.
  BF204.6.D47 2006
  158.1—dc22

                          2005037410

08 07 06

10 9 8 7 6 5 4 3 2 1

First printing

To William M. DeRoo, husband and father,
without whom this never would have happened.

If we can become one-tenth as good at positive self-talk
as we are at negative self-talk, we will notice
an enormous change.

—Julia Cameron, *The Artist's Way*

I believe the lasting revolution comes from deep changes
in ourselves that influence our collective life.

—Anaïs Nin

table of contents

acknowledgments

First and foremost, the authors wish to thank the staff at New Harbinger Publications, in particular Carole Honeychurch, Tesilya Hanauer, and Heather Mitchener for their keen vision for the book's form, invaluable feedback, and consistent encouragement. Deepest gratitude goes to Elsa Hurley of the Candice Fuhrman Agency for her dedication and business acumen.

Thanks go to Andy Couturier and Joan Lester for their cogent advice and enthusiastic support. Thank you to Jeanette Willert for teaching Carolyn how to write.

Many people have contributed ideas, insight, and, in the early stages, much-needed cheerleading for this project. Thank you to Cathy McQueeney, Tess Daniel, Jan Dederick, Nancy Kent, Yoyi Steele, Emily Sandor, Kyle DeRoo, Bill DeRoo, Rebecca DeRoo, Joe Kury, Marcia Feitel, Maureen Pattarelli, Elizabeth Lago, Lori Smullin, Katherine Arthurs, Kathryn Hillgrove, and the Alice Arts Center group.

Carlene wishes to thank Gene Brockopp, the psychologist's psychologist, who has always been there professionally and personally and has encouraged the making of this book.

part
1

laying the foundation

introduction

You need to claim the events of your life and
make them yours. When you truly possess all
you have been and done, which may take some time,
you are fierce with reality. —Florida Scott Maxwell

Question: What is the benefit of recognizing your strengths and appreciating yourself?

Answer: Confidence and self-knowledge. A better life.

Is it any wonder we doubt ourselves to the degree that we do? An axiom of the customer-service industry is that a customer needs to hear seven compliments about a product to counter a single criticism. This is how the human brain works, and it can wreak havoc on how you feel about yourself. But now it's time to get back to reality—a reality in which what is right about us far outweighs what we perceive to be wrong. This reality may be unfamiliar. What would it feel like to live in a world in which harsh judgment was replaced with comfort, and hesitation was replaced with confidence? With a little effort you can find out. Whether you're a parent, salesperson, nun, teenager, CEO, ballet dancer, or therapist, you can enjoy this book and benefit from using it. Some people who are struggling to get by might fear that this kind of self-reflective work is a luxury for those with ample time and resources. But actually, these principles work regardless of class, race, background, gender, or bank balance.

healthy, wealthy, and wise

We are seeing a trend toward a more positive kind of psychology, a shift from "Fix It" to "What's Right with Me." When making life changes, it is more powerful and effective to focus on relevant successes rather than on problems. This shift is reflected in the movement of mainstream psychology toward solution-focused therapy. Solution-focused therapy is a short-term, goal-focused therapeutic approach that helps clients change by emphasizing what they do well regarding a particular issue. Clients apply their energy toward constructing solutions rather than dwelling on problems. Within the last ten years this groundbreaking model has been adopted into mainstream psychology as a powerful tool for healing. Embraced by health-care providers because it yields meaningful results quickly, solution-focused therapy is currently being sought by millions of Americans. Focusing on the solution rather than the problem has been proven to speed the healing process when grappling with any of a breadth of issues. For example, even when there is a long history of substance abuse, treatment, and relapses, focusing on the positive is powerful enough to help people finally free themselves from addiction (Berg and Shafer 2004). Focusing on the positive is the key that gets results, once and for all.

In his book, *Learned Optimism* (1998), Martin Seligman describes the "roots of a positive life" which includes the capacity to love and be loved, creativity, spirituality, courage, wisdom, altruism, and other traits that are considered personality characteristics of one who lives the good (positive) life. Truly being able to love others necessitates loving ourselves and claiming our positive attributes and traits. All through life there are lessons to reflect on

4

and build on as we encounter more challenges. We are not rats in mazes who struggle more valiantly when faced with increased frustration and deprivation. Psychophysiology has proven this for decades. Stress only works as motivation in modest doses. Now we know and understand that most people thrive on praise, kindness, appreciation, compliments, and positive interaction.

a new model

At the Stephen M. Ross School of Business at the University of Michigan, faculty researchers are pioneering a new, highly effective approach to the traditional appraisal and self-improvement processes used by most business organizations. This new alternative emphasizes building upon each person's unique talents and capabilities rather than trying to fix their performance shortfalls. A developmental process called the "Reflected Best Self Exercise" has been integrated into the Ross School of Business curriculum at all levels to help students discover their "best self" and determine ways they create value for other people. Ultimately, the goal is to enable people to become active architects of job activities that utilize and develop their talents and to enrich their relationships with others. This technique arose from the new science of positive organizational scholarship: the study of organizations typified by appreciation and fulfillment (De Groat 2004). Harvard, MIT, Penn State, Stanford, the University of Michigan, Rice, Duke, and Case Western are among the universities now teaching positive organizational scholarship. Why are the top business schools in America teaching their MBAs to develop organizational culture rooted in shared success and acknowledgment of strengths? It increases profits.

writing as medicine

This book requires that you do a lot of thinking and also a lot of writing. We chose this method because many studies show that writing benefits both body and mind. James Pennebaker, the leading researcher in this field, has seen the power of writing among people of all demographics, from children to the elderly, honors students to maximum-security prisoners. Typically, research study participants write for fifteen to thirty minutes a day, for as little as three to five consecutive days. Participants who were encouraged to really let go and explore their deepest emotions had better physical and emotional health in the following months. Control-group members, who were asked to write about superficial topics, did not experience mental or physical health benefits. Even though participants might sometimes cry while writing about charged topics, the overwhelming majority report that the writing experience was valuable and meaningful in their lives (Pennebaker 1997).

Writing benefits your health in profound ways. Writing about significant personal experiences strengthens your immune system and decreases your number of doctor visits. Astonishing behavioral changes have also been found: writing has helped students get better grades and laid-off professionals get new jobs more quickly. When writing from six research studies was analyzed, good health was associated with use of words like "understand," "realize," "because," and "reason" (Pennebaker 1997). Reflection that spurs realization and deep understanding is truly healing.

why we wrote this book

The authors, Carlene and Carolyn, have been working on making their lives and their selves better for a long time. This effort has taken the form of exercise classes, therapy, expensive haircuts, meditation, weepy talks with loved ones, spiritual work, and so on. These things are helpful. But at the same time, we kind of wish we had therapists who focused on the good stuff: what we do well, how beautiful we can be, what good decisions we make. After all, good qualities and actions are a part of everyone, and it's important to acknowledge them. So much of the life-changing business focuses on what is wrong with us, our lives, our thinking, our psyches, and our past.

But this isn't the whole story. We are good people. (Okay, if you are an unreformed violent criminal, ignore that last sentence.) By and large, we make good decisions. We do good things. We really, truly try to have good lives. We're all human: perfectly imperfect. While it's not wrong to want to change or examine one's life, it is equally if not more important to fully recognize what is working and what we want to remain as is.

This book and the process of working through it are not intended to artificially sweeten the hard stuff. The authors are big believers in feeling the uncomfortable feelings: anger, loneliness, sadness, guilt, grief, depression, or anxiety. The work you'll be doing isn't intended to cover up or deny what is difficult. It's intended to provide ballast.

For example, do not stifle feelings that naturally arise if your car breaks down. If you're angry, don't force yourself to think good thoughts about your car. However, at some point after your car gets towed and fixed, spend a moment recognizing and appreciating how you handled the situation. Hey, that part is free!

You will know and like yourself better after you remember and record in this book some good things about yourself. Every compliment counts. Every secret feeling of approval that you have for yourself counts. Acknowledging the good helps us avoid getting lost in our faults. The positive is valid and is every bit as real as the negative.

The good news is that using this book is fun. Self-praise may initially seem awkward, but as you realize that no one is looking over your shoulder, expecting you to be modest, any resistance will vanish and it will feel like a party.

Then, once you have completed this book, you can revisit it when you're feeling down. Did you just have an argument with your sister? Go to the chapter on relationships and reread the nicest thing your sister ever said to you. Focusing on the positive is not the same as repressing anger, fear, sadness, grief, and the like. In addition to feeling painful emotions, it is necessary to your emotional health to feel good things in abundance. You must have a means of reminding yourself of all the reasons why you are good, worthy, wonderful, talented, beautiful, and unique.

about the authors

Dr. Carlene DeRoo and Carolyn DeRoo are a mother and daughter writing team. Throughout their relationship they have enjoyed many conversations about the mind, health, relaxation, and self-knowledge. From these conversations, they have been inspired to develop a book of exercises that not only improve self-esteem but are easy and fun to use.

Carlene saw the benefit of the process used in this book early on in her career. As a clinical psychologist, she was trained to look for pathology. Yet she found that her patients improved faster if she first worked with them on their self-esteem. Looking for positives in themselves and their lives worked in treating people with substance abuse issues that ranged from smoking cessation to hard-drug habits. It also worked with people who had received custodial care for five to twenty-five years in a state mental hospital, not to mention with people seeking help with anxiety or depression. Time and time again, Carlene saw that focusing on the positive in one's self and in one's life increased the ability to make real changes in one's outlook.

Carolyn is a writer who spent five years in Silicon Valley providing technical support to stressed-out computer users. She discovered that focusing on the positive was the quickest way to resolve their issues and reduce their anxiety. Her approach worked. She resolved technical issues 60 percent faster than her coworkers.

The techniques that Carlene and Carolyn used on the job are the basis for *What's Right with Me*. They have seen the overwhelming advantage of affirming an individual's strengths and successes and want to share these highly efficient tools to help people get the confidence and peace of mind that they deserve.

how to use this book

Because this book teaches an internal, reflective process, it's best to use it in a quiet, private space. The last thing you want is to worry that someone is looking over your shoulder and reading what you've written. When you are doing the exercises, if you find yourself eager to stop writing and close the book or wanting to get the writing over with as quickly as possible, then notice your response and compassionately give yourself a break. Take a breath or two and resume, perhaps with a new question (see the activity "A Quick Fix" at the end of chapter 8). Let the experience of answering the questions find its own pace. Be big and bold when writing in this book. There is no danger here. Risk being as honest as you possibly can.

Do not feel that you need to work through the chapters sequentially. Within the first two sections of the book, chapters one through seven, feel free to skip around.

Use full sentences. When prompted to write down a compliment that a relative gave you, do not just write "thoughtful." Write "A relative told me that I was thoughtful." Better yet, "My Aunt Trish told me that I was thoughtful last summer. It made me feel so valued and loved." Invest the time in remembering, recording, and savoring the whole picture. You will be more likely to remember the positive past experience going forward and get a lot more staying power out of the exercise.

If you have a hard time coming up with responses, give yourself time. If you leave a blank, don't panic. It's likely that something will come to mind within the next days or weeks, and you will be able to go back and fill in that space. Memories bubble up from the subconscious when you set your intention toward finding them. If after a couple of weeks there are still some blank spaces, ask a trusted friend for help. She or he will probably help you remember some good things about yourself that may be hard for you to recall.

For example, if you truly cannot think of one good thing that happened to you as a teenager, just leave the space blank. This doesn't mean that you're flawed or less "good" than someone who can fill in that space on the page. Let it go—but stay open to the possibility of remembering something positive about your teenage years in the next few weeks. Sometimes simply surviving a difficult stage in our lives is a brilliant success.

Do not feel that you have to stop writing when you reach the end of this book. Keep the momentum going! You will be likely to have more to write down in the days and weeks following the completion of this book. Hooray! There are fifteen blank pages at the end of this book. When you've filled those, buy a notebook or journal and keep the process rolling. Most of us know only a small fraction of what is right about us. There is a lot for us to discover or rediscover.

Remember, this is your book. No one else ever has to see it, so you can really shine. Flatter yourself. Be true. Do not leave anything out because of modesty. If you want to share your writing with someone else, you can copy it onto a single sheet of paper or read from the book. It can be for your eyes only. It is for no one to judge.

Spelling does not count. Grammar does not count. Just write.

chapter one

getting started

Think of what you have rather than what you lack.
Of the things you have, select the best, and then
reflect how eagerly you would have sought them if
you did not have them. —Marcus Aurelius

shifting focus to the good

So often we focus on the troubles in our lives. Unless we are celebrating a present success—having a housewarming party or going out to dinner to celebrate a new job—when do we spotlight what is going well? When do we ever savor a good choice made last year or ten years ago? We celebrate marriages, births, graduations, birthdays, and retirements. Is that it? How about pausing to appreciate a year of financial solvency or having good medical insurance? How about toasting six months of great sex? Day-to-day things are important, too. What would it feel like to live among a multitude of reasons for joy?

What keeps us from that? We pick up the phone to call a friend when things go wrong and we need support. Or we ask a child in college if

> *We have been taught to believe that negative equals realistic and positive equals unrealistic.* —Susan Jeffers

everything is all right, anticipating a report of the challenges and catastrophes that are defining life. When the ship is sinking, we reach out. What about when it's smooth sailing? What about being able to say, "I'm going to sleep, waking up, buying the groceries, going to work, paying the bills, and everything is going along just fine"? It is a great thing to have both the big and the mundane in your life falling into place. When chatting with friends or family, we can choose to talk about all of the things that are going well in life: a productive meeting or a sweet moment with your partner. Again, this does not mean ignoring tears or anger that you might be feeling. The idea is breaking a habit of connecting with others through focusing on what's going wrong. You will be delighted at the gentle lift you'll feel from seeing the positives revealed in your life when you focus on the smooth waters and steady breeze.

the benefits of looking at the positive

Your work in this book will strengthen your self-esteem. Seeing your strengths written down in black and white brings a solidity and reality to your life experiences. Truths spelled out in words are powerful. Knowing your talents, strengths, and accomplishments and having the ability to articulate them clearly will help you feel more confident in all areas of your life, as well as in specific situations. As you write in this book, you will develop ease in articulating your talents. Owning compliments that are true and justified will start to feel more natural and less awkward. You will feel more confident not only when interviewing for a job but also when asking someone out on a date, but any time you are approaching a challenging situation or facing a major decision. The process of using this book will give you fuel to get what you want out of life.

> *Happiness is the whole aim and end of human existence.*
> —Aristotle

Increased confidence can help you:

- Feel more calm and happy,

- Feel less depressed or anxious,

- Feel confident,

- Get what you want,

- Take risks,

- Be assertive,

- Make better choices that align with your own goals and desires,

- Take on new projects,

- Be more intimate,

- Develop a better body image,

- Appreciate your partner or family, and

- Replace patterns and behaviors that don't serve you well (even if you are not fully conscious of them).

This self-knowledge can provide countless other benefits. Furthermore, as your confidence grows, your ability to enjoy life will increase. You can feel safer and more optimistic if you feel powerful in creating what you want. In short, after completing this book, you can expect to feel stronger, and that feeling will permeate all areas of your life.

staying positive during hard times

Although this book is useful anytime, it is particularly helpful when dealing with adversity. Are you in a tough work situation? Are you going through a breakup? Is there someone in your life who is harsh and critical? Do you want more vitality in your marriage? Are you looking for a job or considering a career change? Have you had a business or creative setback? Or do you simply want to feel better about yourself? Nurture yourself by working through this book.

Increased self-awareness and confidence is crucial in difficult times. For example, when a relationship or job is not going well, where do you find the courage and inspiration to move on? You may remember a friend telling you that she feels like she has to settle for a mediocre relationship. Although on an intellectual level she knows different, she *feels* inadequate. Underneath her confusion is the question, "Why would someone want me?" Why *would* someone want her? Why would someone want to be her friend, hire her as a teacher, or lend her money for a down payment on a home? This book provides plenty of opportunities to answer those questions with honesty and power. If you can say out loud and write down what is right about you, what makes you worthy, you can attract or ask for what you want and get it.

To make decisions that will work for you, decisions must be based on who you really are and what you really want. To resolve difficulty in a way that makes life better, you need a healthy sense of self. Using this book to look within will foster deep self-knowledge. Challenges of any kind are more easily met when you have a strong sense of self-esteem. Through reflection, seeing the good that you have done and the good that you are, your self-esteem will flourish. Although the process of writing down good things about ourselves can feel delicious in the short term as we do it, there is a

> *The universe is made of stories, not of atoms.*
> —Muriel Rukeyser

long-term benefit to our sense of self-esteem as well. It is this long-term healing and growth that is the real fruit of your labor. This is lasting change, and it does make life better.

getting comfortable with praise

Shifting focus toward the good in your self and your life is rewarding, but it may feel new and unfamiliar at first, especially when the focus is on yourself. Praising yourself or receiving praise from others can feel foreign, even wrong—especially for women. So first get comfortable praising yourself, then try opening to receive praise from others. It seems we are all socialized to fear seeming arrogant. The ancient Greeks shunned bragging because they feared the envy of the gods. We no longer believe in Zeus or Athena, yet we might fear seeming too proud in the eyes of God if we say (or even think) we are good at something. We react similarly if someone else does. What would be your reaction were you to hear a coworker say, "I love how I handled that meeting! I was really on!" or, were you to say, "I look great tonight." Do such statements strike you as inappropriate or arrogant?

confidence versus arrogance

The truth is, feeling good about yourself does not cause arrogance. In fact, it's just the opposite. Insecurity can cause a need to prove yourself to others. The bigger the insecurity, the bigger the desire to brag and show off. Honestly and comfortably acknowledging your abilities, strengths, and beauty leaves you without a need to compensate for a perceived lack. Feeling you have to make up for something that is flawed or missing is what rouses arrogance, and it disconnects you from others. True confidence opens you up to let others in and allows you to honor and acknowledge their achievements and beauty as well.

> *The secret of being free is to remember.*
> —Traditional German saying

The positive cannot hurt you, but it certainly can feel uncomfortable when it comes to you in the form of praise from others. Angela, a television producer, accepts commendations on the job with ease. Yet when she is with friends outside of work, especially those with less glamorous jobs, she quickly changes the subject if one of them begins to congratulate her on her successes. Whenever Josh receives praise from others, he deflects it by pointing out what he does not yet have or who he has not yet become, rarely enjoying all the positives in himself and in his life right now. Little day-to-day satisfactions are easy for some to claim, while glory from larger achievements feels embarrassing. Others easily relish big wins yet overlook smaller tasks done well. Still others can own achievements, as long as they benefit others. This book is not about identifying your top three achievements. It is an ever-evolving inventory of the good you do and the good you are, of crowning moments and everyday good choices. As you practice acknowledging your positives, any discomfort will diminish. Your natural beauty and goodness have been covered with layers of "shoulds" and "becauses." As you grow stronger in claiming and celebrating your "cans" and "dos" and "ams," like the sun burning away clouds, the power of the positive will release needless restrictions.

As you work your way through the exercises in this book, you might feel alarmed by a sudden sense of power or just plain happiness. Do not be fooled. You're not in danger. This is what confidence can feel like. You are revealing yourself to yourself. You are not proving yourself to your partner, your mother, your best friend, or your boss. This is about opening your eyes to the reality of your own greatness. In his 1994 inaugural speech, Nelson Mandela quoted Marianne Williamson on this topic, saying,

Our deepest fear is not that we are inadequate. Our deepest fear is that we are powerful beyond measure. It is our light, not our darkness that most frightens us. We ask ourselves, "Who am I to be brilliant, gorgeous, talented, and fabulous?" Actually, who are you not to be? You are a child of God; your playing small doesn't serve the world. There is nothing enlightening about shrinking so that other people won't feel insecure around you. We were born to make manifest the glory of God that is within us. It is not just some of us: it's everyone. And as we let our own light shine, we unconsciously give others permission to do the same. As we are liberated from our own fear, our presence automatically liberates others.

Living with great self-confidence is a service to others. If you knew that letting yourself be seen as smart and talented would help others feel more confident, what old, negative thinking could you let go?

Now, let's move on to the heart of this book, fun exercises where you get to focus on what's right with you. You will start by identifying some of the things that you do well. Feel free to draw on the past when responding to these questions. When noting something that you cook well, for instance, do not feel guilty if you haven't cooked a six-course dinner party for twelve lately. One woman described a beautifully decorated birthday cake that she had baked for her father twenty years ago. Was it difficult or complicated? No. Yet it conjured one of her warmest family memories. If you make scrambled eggs well, then write that down. An everyday plate of delicious scrambled eggs is just as worthwhile as a glamorous baked Alaska. Resist the urge to rate your fortes. Ignore the naysaying voice that says, "It was no big deal." Value what you do well.

Your words create what you speak about.
Learn to speak positively. —Sanaya Roman

17

What two things do you secretly believe you are good at but never tell anyone? Are you a great kisser, for instance? Good at math or driving around curves?

_____

_____

_____

_____

_____

_____

What have you invested time in exploring? Nutrition? Sailing? Civil War history? Spirituality?

_____

_____

_____

_____

_____

_____

> *If we [women] were to actually cut, even by a quarter, the amount of money and the amount of time we spend fixing ourselves, do you know what the planet would be like?*
> —Eve Ensler

For what have you worked very hard?

_____

_____

_____

_____

_____

What aspects of you do others appreciate? Do people often tell you that you have a good sense of humor? Are people amazed at your patience?

_____

_____

_____

_____

_____

Think of a time when you said yes to something that you wanted, even if it meant some sacrifice or complication.

_____

_____

_____

_____

_____

> *Maybe your discomfort signals not what's wrong but,
> rather, what's right with you. Why not ask yourself
> how you adjust to a social structure that teaches you
> to beat up on your natural self?* —Judi Hollis

Write down one physical activity that you are good at. You can call yourself a good swimmer even if you haven't been in a pool in years.

_____

_____

Recall a creative capability. Do you make crafts, cultivate a garden, paint, or raise children?

_____

_____

Record a social skill that you possess. Are you good at staying in touch with friends or putting people at ease?

_____

_____

Which self-care activities do you do? Do you exercise regularly? Do you get therapy when you need it?

_____

_____

Think of a risk you took that paid off.

_____

_____

_____

_____

_____

_____

Write about one "bad habit" you have that someone else has appreciated. This should be something that is not injurious to you or others. Do others giggle when you barge into rooms and then ask if it's okay to come in?

_____

_____

_____

_____

_____

_____

_____

> _I pray for peaceful pauses within ourselves to acknowledge our gratitude for life and all its complexities._
> —Oprah Winfrey

> *It is in the knowledge of the genuine conditions of our lives that we must draw our strength to live and our reasons for living.* —Simone de Beauvoir

Look back on a compassionate act or a moment of understanding toward yourself or another. What did you do? What enabled you to do it?

_____

_____

_____

_____

_____

When have you surprised yourself with your own courage?

_____

_____

_____

_____

_____

activity: your symbol of success

Recall an achievement that felt like a real win, a "hit the home run that won the game" moment. When have you shouted, "Yes!" and punched your fist into the air? Close your eyes and take a moment to savor that feeling. Is there an image that might represent this moment? Create a simple drawing of your symbol. If no symbols immediately come to mind, look through some magazines and see if any images resonate with you. Or, revisit a photo album. You might even want to create an abstract symbol to represent the moment. Add an appropriate word if it feels right. This is your symbol of success. If you are more auditory, perhaps a piece of music comes to mind. Use a word or visual representation to remind yourself of it.

One man simply tore a picture of a cigarette in half and glued the two pieces onto a sheet of paper. After years of battling with smoking he had finally quit for good. His winning moment was realizing that he had been cigarette free for two years. The broken cigarette perfectly symbolized his victory over a powerful addiction. One woman used a close-up photo of her dog's face to remind her of rescuing the beloved pet from the pound. At that point in her life, she needed to see that she was caring and giving. Another woman remembered the day that she moved into her first apartment. She drew a picture of the key, which symbolized independence and stability. A father recalled the pride he felt when his daughter was born and drew a picture of her tiny hand in his. Place your symbol somewhere where you will see it often, such as on your nightstand or on a cabinet door. As you see it in passing, it will aid in shifting your day-to-day thoughts toward the positive.

taking stock

Notice that you are not making anything up. As you look back at your responses, know that all of these wonderful recollections you are writing are facts. You can write in detail, you can write descriptively, you can write with soul. But you will never need to make up an ability. You will never need to fabricate a memory of success. Right now, in your life history, you have the answers to all the questions in this book. In completing these tasks, only your self-image may have to change.

You did some real work in this chapter, and even though it's fun, it takes time and energy. Give yourself credit for slowing down and resisting any urges you may have had to skip through the process with the quickest possible answers. Slowing down brings the openness that results in the most meaningful memories. As you wrote in this chapter, you began to get used to saying "I am good at..." and "People like that I am..." and "My talents are..." You are beginning to get what you came for in using this book. This self-knowledge will be reflected in your life in many ways. The means may be invisible, but the results are visible. You might notice that others treat you differently, perhaps listen to you more respectfully. You may feel more empowered to take a risk or feel more physically attractive. You might simply feel more at ease. Whatever the shift, completing the exercises in this chapter has illuminated formerly hidden strengths, talents, and skills. As the fog lifts, trust what you're seeing. Trust that the amazing person being revealed is you—the real you.

> *Not only have we achieved victories, we have—despite the*
> *powers against us—become our own victories.*
> —Camille Crosby

24

timelines: seeing your core self

You need to claim the events of your life to make
yourself yours. —Anne Wilson-Schaef

you've already got what you're looking for

A friend tells me that as a four-year-old, she climbed onto a stack of six phone books so that she could reach something high on a bookshelf. Reprimanded by her frightened mother for being reckless, my friend learned instantly that her determination could get her into big trouble. Her conclusion: temper that determination, hide it, beware of it. Now a lively and creative forty-three-year-old woman, she longs to find within herself the commitment to develop a fine-art business that she has dreamed of for years. Though content with her marriage, friendships, and finances, she has never felt deeply fulfilled at work. Lacking the drive to pursue her artistic dream, she spent twenty years building a safe and steady career as a pharmacist. She longed to realize the determination necessary to drive her toward her true work, yet was unaware that this quality already existed within her. After reflecting on some childhood experiences, she recovered awareness of her natural strength. When her fierce determination resurfaced, she was able to use it to take the steps toward opening a gallery. Could you have some trait that was forced down or frightened into invisibility? Is it possible that you already possess what you are longing to be?

re-writing history

Many of us have learned how to censor our strengths. To access them again, we need to mine for them, to overturn the stones of fear or habit and uncover the riches still inside us. This chapter provides an opportunity for you to look back at your life and recover those strengths that you expressed in the past, yet for some reason went underground. This chapter also offers an opportunity to reshape your conception of your life history, to reclaim the thread of positive experiences rather than acknowledging only the negative. The path your life takes is affected by both, yet the negative experiences tend to stand out in our minds as the true shapers of our lives. This can lead to thinking that the past has largely been series of struggles in which you were not sufficiently supported by others or by life. We must acknowledge the trials we have survived and grieve as our souls direct us. Yet we must also see the gifts we have received: the generosity, the opportunities, and the support. The danger of bleak memories overtaking our history is that we expect more of the same for the future.

Ana, a technical-support manager, held a position that required her to speak to groups of clients and coworkers. Outdoorsy and adventurous, she spent her weekends hiking with her best friend or alone with her dog. Although she was willing, every time Ana found herself ready to speak to a

> *Time does not change us. It just unfolds us.* —Max Frisch

> *The route through childhood is shaped by many forces,*
> *and it differs for each of us.* —Robert Wozniak

group, she felt overwhelming anxiety. She took workshops on public speaking and read every book she could find on the topic. Believing that a traumatic childhood event must be the cause of her stress, Ana scoured her psyche—to no avail. Through answering the questions in this chapter, she was able to look back on her childhood with gentleness, simply to see what *was*, not necessarily what was difficult. Instead of a demon, to her surprise, she found a jack-in-the-box.

In third grade, Ana had been asked to lead her class in reciting the Pledge of Allegiance. She had never stood before her class alone. Her mind went blank. After an uncomfortable pause, she asked, "How does it go again?" Her classmates roared. Ana soon realized they were not laughing at her but at what they heard as a brilliant joke. Continuing to reflect, Ana recalled how she hammed up funny skits with her cousins at family gatherings. She recalled how eagerly she took her turn reading morning announcements over her junior high school public address system. Recognizing that she had fun in front of groups as a child gave Ana a renewed sense of possibility as an adult, and helped her relax. Within weeks, much of her anxiety about public speaking had abated, and Ana even began to look forward to speaking before groups. Looking back at what you did well or enjoyed as a child can provide you with epiphanies relevant to your current life challenges.

Praise or Shame?

In childhood, cleverness and creativity often help us get what we want: our older sibling's stuff, sweets, or an extra fifteen minutes of television before going to bed. Anyone who has tried to negotiate with a determined three-year-old knows the creative force of that will when she truly wants something. As we grow older, we are taught to heed the guidance of our caregivers, usually offered in the service of our safety, but sometimes at the expense of trusting our own intuitive abilities and resourcefulness. While children's lives depend on parental guidance, as adults we must reclaim aspects of ourselves that were repressed, however inadvertently.

One very successful charity fund-raiser recalls her achievement selling tacky change purses for a junior high school sale. "My older sister was labeled 'The Popular One,'" she remembered. "My younger sister was 'The Pretty One.' Even at the age of eleven, I could sell cases and cases of those awful purses. I guess I was 'The Persuasive One.'" She has a skill that now serves her and her community. In fact, her persuasive abilities in fund-raising put her in great demand. What might have happened if she had not been rewarded for this skill as a child? What if she had been shamed? Those of us who were not duly rewarded for our gifts must now take up the task of valuing them.

If we look back at our lives with curiosity and kindness, we might be startled at our bravery. Often, we are taken aback by our natural propensity as children to explore what we truly enjoyed. Before a child learns what is acceptable in her environment, she is clear on how she wants to spend her time. If she wants to create her own play and perform it for her block, she will. What four-year-old wakes up thinking, "How on earth am I going to make it through my day?" At fourteen, she eagerly participates in a talent show. Will she at forty? The truth is, we are still as brave, creative, and determined as we were at two, twelve, or twenty. We just need to remember our resources. It might take a little time to see ourselves fully, but with some examination, our natural gifts and fascinations will emerge. Let your soul gravitate to what it truly loves. Be willing to know what it is you truly love to do and what you truly do well. Often, they are the same.

I think self-awareness is probably the most important thing towards being a champion. —Billie Jean King

Connect the Dots

When a few past events are written down side by side, as they will be in this chapter, connections may appear. For example, Lourdes did not see herself as athletic. Now a microbiology professor, she had always focused on her academic and intellectual identity. Yet when she listed the activities for which she was rewarded as a child, several images surfaced: the small plastic trophy her gym teacher gave her for floor tumbling; the paper certificates she received each year at her school's bike rodeo; and a cherished tennis racquet, reminding her of her solid record on the high school team. She had always told herself that she did athletic things as a kid only because her friends did them. By the age of thirty-seven, feeling out of shape and lethargic, she felt intimidated about joining a gym. Then she looked at the facts. Was she an Olympic hopeful? No. Did she have some demonstrated athletic ability? Yes. But, having been buried by time, gender expectations, and modesty, it was not apparent. Knowing that she had real ability sparked Lourdes'motivation to join a gym and improve her health and energy level. Her memories bolstered her courage to try something new.

Trying new things is a huge, and often enjoyable, component of childhood. From climbing a step to dialing a telephone or petting a dog, the risk inherent in new experience is everywhere a child turns. As you grew older, you risked seeing the world differently than your family members and friends. Your efforts may have been embraced, rejected, or ignored by those around you. That reaction, or lack of one, affected you. More specifically, it affected how you saw yourself. What risks did you take? What got you into trouble? How might the same attributes that got you into trouble as a child serve you constructively as an adult?

You don't get to choose how you're going to die, or when.
You can only decide how you're going to live now.
—Joan Baez

29

> *Freedom is what you do with what's been done to you.*
> —Jean-Paul Sartre

The questions below only require short answers. They are intended to begin a process of self-discovery about some of your long-buried character traits and strengths.

What activities did you enjoy when growing up?

Between the ages of one and five, I really enjoyed

_____

When I did it I felt

_____

Between the ages of six and eleven, I really enjoyed

_____

When I did it I felt

_____

Between the ages of twelve and fifteen, I really enjoyed

_____

When I did it I felt

_____

Between the ages of sixteen and nineteen, I really enjoyed

_____

When I did it I felt

_____

Now I really enjoy

_____

When I do it I feel

_____

As a child, what made you feel alive, confident, or like your true self? Did you make a good friend, win a contest, or have an occasion to be the center of attention?

Elementary school

_____

_____

Junior high

_____

_____

High school

_____

_____

> _As people grow up they cease to play and they seem to give up the yield of pleasure which they gain from playing._
> —Sigmund Freud

> *We must be willing to get rid of the life we've planned, so as to have the life that is waiting for us.*
> —Joseph Campbell

Recall some accomplishments from different stages of life. What made you feel like you were good at something?

From your teenage years

_____

_____

As a young adult

_____

_____

From mid-life

_____

_____

As an older adult

_____

_____

> *Time is nature's way of preventing everything from happening at once.* —Unknown

What did you like about yourself at different ages, both when you were at that age and upon reflection now?

As a child. Creativity? Bravery? Determination?

_____

_____

As a teenager. Curiosity? Rebelliousness?

_____

_____

During your twenties and thirties. Ability to fend for yourself? Interest in spirituality? Ability to grow?

_____

_____

As a person in midlife. Ability to shape your own life? Tenacity?

_____

_____

As an older adult. An ability to let go of expectations? A heightened sense of humor? Inner peace?

_____

_____

All men should strive to learn before they die what they are running from, and to, and why. —James Thurber

I will survive

What do you do if you get a knot in your stomach thinking, "Nothing good happened when I was fifteen. My parents got divorced. That was an awful year!"?

First, acknowledge what it took to survive that time, or another. What kept you from losing your mind? Did you play a record over and over because it expressed something that you felt? Maybe you had an ability to really feel your anger. Did you vent for hours on the phone with your best friend? This trait should not be taken lightly; not everyone can feel anger. Some people spend a lot of money on psychotherapy to help them get in touch with anger. Being able to feel an uncomfortable feeling is of great benefit to your psyche and your health. Take a minute to think about how you survived an awful period in your life. During these times we may not collect any trophies. We show our strength through coping.

What did you do to survive a difficult time?

_____

_____

_____

_____

_____

_____

> *The most important skill is the capacity to learn from individual experiences, our own and others.*
> —Edward Shapiro and Wesley Carr

What skills do you use to get through adversity?

_____

_____

_____

_____

_____

_____

a helping hand

Next, ask yourself if there was one moment, person, or conversation during that difficult time that helped. For example, Sara, a nursing student, has an aversion to looking back at her life between the ages of six and twelve. When doing an exercise in this chapter, she remembered being eight years old, wearing a fairy costume while standing in front of her grandmother's house. She heard the swish of the gossamer skirts, saw the glittery wand, felt the hot summer sun on her face, caught a whiff of eucalyptus, and once more listened to the sound of cicadas. Stunned at the fullness of the memory as she relived the magic of the afternoon, she recalled just how significant her grandmother's role had been during those turbulent years. In recognizing how this dear woman cared for Sara consistently during her childhood, she felt supported not only by her grandmother, but by life. That modest but solid increase in optimism helped Sara feel more confident as she ventured into adulthood.

> *Men can be human, with human frailties,*
> *and still be great.* —Stephen Richards

> *Men can starve from a lack of self-realization as much as they can from a lack of bread.* —Richard Wright

Think of a goal, desire, or dream that you have. Recall a compliment that you received between the ages of one and twenty that points to an ability relating to this dream. Who saw who you were and said so? Did friends, teachers, or coaches admire particular abilities?

_____

_____

_____

_____

_____

Who gave you the compliment? Describe her face, how you remember his posture, or the sound of her voice. Do you remember this person with a devilish smile? Where were you when you received this compliment? Was the air warm, cold, fragrant, crisp? What was the light like? Did you tell anyone?

_____

_____

_____

_____

_____

What got you into trouble when growing up? Persistence? Intelligence? Curiosity? Rebellion? How might these attributes serve you positively now?

_____

_____

_____

_____

What do you like about yourself now that was hard to like in the past? Your creativity? Your height? Your sexual expression?

_____

_____

_____

_____

What experience did you not like when you were growing up that gave you a skill you value now? For example, Evan grew up in a suburb of Columbus, Ohio. His neighborhood had streams for jumping across, hills for sledding, and miles of sidewalks for roller-skating. With few responsibilities at

> *We think we have to be flawless. It's not true. You can be sad and still be strong for being able to show that emotion.*
> —Alicia Keys

home, Evan and his friends spent every afternoon together, playing outdoors. Evan's childhood friend, Patrick, had hemophilia. Evan and his other friends often included Patrick during their playtime together, though Patrick's parents forbade him to do many physical activities. As a rambunctious child, Evan sometimes got frustrated with Patrick's limits and wanted to just go adventuring with his other friends. Yet now, as an adult, Evan has a gift for hearing people's needs, even when they seem inconvenient. He is better at his job as a social worker because of challenges like these he met during his childhood.

Do you have a skill that emerged from a challenge during childhood? Maybe you gained an edge from tedious chores. For example, Sandy knows how to pack a suitcase so that nothing wrinkles, prevent moths from picnicking on the clothing in her closet, and prevent nasty smells from contaminating her refrigerator. She learned these skills by grumbling through household chores as a child. The activities are still tedious, but today she appreciates that her skills save her money and aggravation.

What have you gained from a childhood challenge?

_____

_____

_____

_____

_____

> *Man is asked to make of himself what he is supposed to become to fulfill his destiny.* —Paul Tillich

What life skills did you learn as a child? How to be a good friend? How to prepare meals?

_____

_____

_____

_____

_____

patterns

Look back at each group of questions and responses. Do you see any themes within the groups? For example, you may see that you've always shown strength in being kind to others, or you've always been good at sports. But remember, your positive history is worthwhile whether or not themes emerge as you look back.

Are there any themes among the activities you enjoyed at different ages? Is there any similarity in how you felt when doing these things?

_____

_____

_____

> *All of life is the exercise of risk.* —William Sloan Coffin

> [When asked late in life why he was studying geometry]
> *If I should not be learning now, when should I be?*
> —Lacydes

Are there any common factors between what you have liked about yourself at different ages?

_____

How do your accomplishments relate to one another?

_____

Do you see any similarities between the themes?

_____

What positive qualities or abilities are expressed over and over throughout your life?

_____

_____

Are there any positive qualities or abilities that have increased or grown stronger throughout your life?

_____

_____

activity: before and after

Pick the answer to a question from anywhere in the chapter that appeals to you the most. Notice what appeals to you about it. Do you feel comfort from acknowledging a strength or perhaps pride in an unexpected area? How could this comfort or pride be symbolized? If comfort is most appealing to you, what conjures up comfort for you? Any of these things, and others, could symbolize comfort: your old blue jeans, a "Do Not Disturb" sign, your cat, a bookmark, or a fresh bagel. Your symbol does not need to relate to the particular question from the chapter. Perhaps your old blue jeans evoke memories of reading novels in your backyard hammock, or perhaps you just feel a sense of comfort at the thought of wearing them. Close your eyes and find a symbol that feels right to you. Where in your life do you want more of this quality or trait? You will be taking a mental snapshot of this area of your life, then adding your symbol to this picture.

Here's one example from Alisha, a woman who wrote about comfort when responding to several questions. She picked her cat as her comfort symbol. A high-energy marketing manager, Alisha is also a thirty-eight-year-old mother of two small boys. Although she shares home and family responsibilities with a supportive husband, she winds up feeling harried most of the time. She wanted more calm at work at 4 P.M., the most stressful time in her day, when calls from an office in another time zone always flood her phone. If she is unable to answer them, they fill her voice mail in-box. Her throat tightens as she anticipates having to rush to catch up the following morning. Meanwhile, she is racing with the clock to finish her workday and be on time to pick up her kids from day care. To add comfort to this scene, she pictures her cat sitting on top of her desk. Specifically, she sees him lazily licking his paw, unconcerned at the panic swirling around him. Alisha hears the quiet rasp of the cat's tongue, smells the earthy scent of his fur, and imagines his body warming the surface of the desk beneath him. There is a before and after aspect to the images she chose. In the first, stormy winds blow through the office, rustling papers and agitating her. Blinded by hair blowing in her face, she is lunging toward the ringing phone, guided only by sound. In the second image, adding the cat to her scene, the air becomes still and peaceful. Sun shines through the windows, warming the back of her head. The room is quiet.

By transposing feelings of comfort onto a life situation where she is hungry for it, she is changing her relationship to her late-afternoon workday. As she retouches her mental snapshot associations with that time and place, they now include comfort, because they include an image of a cat on her desk. Without realizing it, Alisha's expectations shift. Her new mental picture begins to reshape her present reality. When you find the right symbol, this is an extremely powerful exercise.

Now that you have an idea of how this visualization works, think of an area of your life where you want more of your chosen trait or quality.

1. Choose your symbol.

2. Imagine your "before" clearly. Take one image of it as a mental snapshot. Notice the position of your body, the light, the feel of your energy, the feel of the energy in the environment.

3. Now place the symbol in the center of that scene. Smile to yourself as you see the details of your symbol: its color, texture, temperature, scent, and sound. Take a deep breath and let your shoulders relax. Feel the comfort that it brings you. Notice how you feel inside as you gaze at your symbol and your "after" scene.

Complete this exercise when you have a half an hour of quiet time. Then repeat your visualization once a day when you have a quiet moment. Repetition solidifies the shift in your emotional state in your chosen situation.

To reinforce the mental image after initially completing the exercise, describe it in words. Writing down your "after" scene is extremely important. Documenting your new mental snapshot will cement the fresh image in your memory. Also, writing your "after" scene clarifies the components of the scene, making it easier to repeat the visualization after a day or two has passed. Reread your scene before you visualize to bring the images into sharp focus. Rereading also ensures that you remember each precious aspect and include them when you visualize. You can edit and enhance your scene as you are inspired, bearing in mind that if significant changes are made, some repetition of this new scene will be required. The stronger it takes root mentally, the greater the shift in your experience.

_____

_____

_____

_____

_____

_____

_____

the past as a path

By revisiting different times in your life, you have excavated parts of yourself. Bringing those positive aspects to the surface so that you can see them, you are better able to trust the long-held secret feeling that you would be a great entrepreneur, that you are a talented drummer, or that you really do have a bold side. In the before and after activity, you transposed a quality that called to you, growing its presence in your life. Tapping your creativity to conjure an appealing after, you changed your reality.

You are brave for revisiting times in your life that may have been laced or loaded with pain. Your history is like no one else's, and it has honed you. Also, you have risked feeling sentimental, which is often sweet tinged with sour: longing, missing loved ones, and engaging in questioning that reflection can spur. The rewards are many: delighting in strengths, realizing talents, and discovering support from others that you didn't see before. Whatever your dreams are, you likely have a track record that supports success in making them a reality.

This was a lengthy and involved chapter. It has left you with a lot of gifts. Appreciate the volume of work that you have done, and treasure the riches you have gleaned. Allow this new but completely real knowledge to become part of your self-image. As tempting as it is to write off your abilities to do, create, or survive, you deserve to get the benefit of the work you have just done. Trust what you've uncovered.

It is good to have an end to journey towards; but it is the journey that matters, in the end. —Ursula K. Le Guin

concrete evidence

We use the past to define ourselves, to deal with the present, and to prepare for the future. Memory dictates the way we express ourselves, think about ourselves, and communicate with others; it is the core of being human.
—Edith Nalle Schafer

creating an accurate memory

The reality of your life is better than you think. You are more capable than you know. The disconnect between what is true and what we think comes from two things: how the brain processes perceptions and memories, and erroneous self-talk.

Memory is like the background noise in our heads as we go through life. Memory tells us what reality looks like, but is it accurate? The loss of a job might seem overwhelming enough to totally undo us. We might feel great anxiety, if not all-out horror. Of course, these feelings are normal and should be allowed to flow through to their release. At the same time, how might it change the experience to recall even one of these true statements?

- In the end, I am good at dealing with transition—even when it is unexpected and feels uncomfortable.

- I did good work at this job and I have a good reputation.

- The last time a big, scary, unexpected event happened in my life, it led to a good outcome.

- I have always been able to make ends meet, even when I was really broke.

The purpose of using the exercises in this book is to become infused with courage and a sense of power in shaping the conditions of your life. Some benefits are immediate: a change in self-image or sense of control over your circumstances. Deeply rewarding but less direct, another benefit is an increased ease in being your authentic self so that the life you want unfolds naturally. It's amazing how powerful it is to remember hidden facts about our lives that are positive—facts that reflect that we are intelligent, kind, strong people.

To illustrate this, let's take an example of a woman needing a career change. Barbara is deathly bored with her job and wants to go into a totally new line of work. She never really liked any of her jobs and feels frustrated and overwhelmed at the thought of finding enjoyable work: "How will I ever find work that I like? It's impossible." When she thinks back on her work history, her memory is limited by her perception: "I have never had a good job. Work is boring." Memory feeds back sound bites into internal self-talk; these sound-bite beliefs then become set-in-stone reality. Unless Barbara consciously looks for things that she is not remembering—praise from her manager, good talks with a work friend—she will not see the more complex

The choices we make determine who we become, offering
us the possibility of leading an authentic life.
—Jean Shinoda Bolen

reality of her work history, which includes some good. The brain tends to generalize experiences into manageable categories of memory. Thus, if you have many bad experiences at a certain job, it later becomes difficult to remember any good times there. Important details can be buried. This book is a guide to exploring the aggregated memories that can make change seem so difficult.

If Barbara sees only a series of past jobs that were unfulfilling, she would need superhuman strength to forge ahead, fighting with all of her might toward fulfilling work. Rather than dragging around her work history like a lead weight, she can ease the struggle by taking a moment to review the past and look for hidden facts. What aspects of her former jobs has she liked? Perhaps a few coworkers became good friends, or she had the respect of others for doing good work. Maybe she had a job or two that paid really well. Once she realizes a few small treasures amidst what was assumed to be all trash, the gap between what she has and what she wants shortens. She no longer needs superstrength to fight her way from a grim "reality" comprised of nothing but awful experiences. Nor is her only option for action an impossibly huge leap from a hopeless situation into a great one.

It is natural that anyone might feel some frustration or anxiety when contemplating a major life change. Instead of trying to fix yourself in some way ("If only I were____, then I'd have a great job"), it is more powerful and immediate to mine your memory for buried facts. A little knowledge based on fact recognition is enough to upset extreme all-or-nothing thinking and remind you that you have what it takes to get what you need.

self-talk: the things you tell yourself

In addition to perception and memory, self-talk has a hand in shaping how people see themselves, their abilities, and their limitations. Brains are very busy. Not only do you have a lot of new information to process throughout the day, you have millions of pieces of learned information that inform your experience from moment to moment. Generally, people don't focus on the

> *What lies behind us and what lies before us are tiny*
> *matters compared to what lies within us.*
> —Ralph Waldo Emerson

messages themselves but instead focus on accomplishing a task at hand: driving a car, making a sandwich, calling a friend. Self-talk is a component of all of this thinking. Self-talk is how you talk to yourself about yourself. It can sound like "Oh, stupid me, I forgot to mail that letter" or "I look great today, and everyone will notice it." These thoughts occur so quickly that you probably don't even perceive them as sentences. Yet you go about thinking thoughts that either build you up or tear you down.

The unconscious mind hears these thoughts and uses them to create experience that reflects these beliefs. If you believe that life is a struggle, then life will be hard. If you believe that flying on airplanes is scary, then it will be. The subconscious mind does not know what is true and what is false. All it knows is what it is told. It believes you if you tell it that the earth rotates around the sun. It believes you if you tell it that you are not smart enough. The subconscious receives thoughts as facts.

Looking to History

You can look at your own life history for proof that you already have some of what you want to expand or experience more fully. Michelle is a thirty-three-year-old woman with a stable job. She hoped to save money to buy a house. However, it seemed that no matter how much money she made, she couldn't manage to save. This led her to believe that she was bad with money. If Michelle felt that she wanted to spend money more appropriately, in ways that genuinely served her life, she could recall two or three good financial decisions that she has made. For example, if she recalled that she paid her car loan off on time and contributed to her company's retirement plan for five years, the picture she has of herself changes. She is not bad with money, inept, guilty, and so on. She has made some really good decisions. After writing down these positive choices, she will begin to focus on the positive history, and her self-image will change. Then, feeling more relaxed about money, she will remember even more good financial decisions, further boosting her self-image and confidence. Best of all, Michele will begin spending her money in ways that serve her highest good. When you upset all-or-nothing thinking, such as "I'm bad with money," by introducing a few positive facts, self-image changes and a sense of possibility opens. The only effort you need to expend is recalling the facts.

Once you open your memory just a crack and let a positive fact into your consciousness, you have a catalyst for growth. As you consciously accept your skills and abilities, you gain a huge amount of confidence. This process empowers you to change any behavior or situation, to align with the life you truly want.

In this chapter you'll take stock of actual events and experiences that you lived and created. What you will recall and write in this chapter are real, tangible, physical examples of what you have done and do well. Enjoy the reality check!

What good financial decisions have you made? Push yourself to list as many as you can. Have you invested in education, paid off a loan, or stayed afloat despite immense challenges?

_____

_____

_____

_____

_____

_____

> *Knowing others is intelligence; knowing*
> *yourself is true wisdom. —Tao Te Ching*

List two times when you said something funny that made the people around you laugh.

_____

_____

_____

_____

_____

Think of a few good things that you have done for other people.

_____

_____

_____

_____

_____

_____

When have you encouraged someone else?

_____

_____

_____

_____

_____

List a few good things that you have done for yourself. For example, do you allow yourself relaxation and downtime? Have you insisted on a fair child-support agreement?

_____

_____

_____

_____

_____

_____

You have the power in the present moment to change limiting beliefs and consciously plant the seeds for the future of your choosing. As you change your mind, you change your experience. —Serge Kahili King

What are the best decisions you have made?

_____

_____

_____

_____

_____

When have you gracefully admitted defeat? How did it benefit you
in the long run?

_____

_____

_____

_____

_____

When have you asked a question even though you felt shy?

_____

_____

_____

_____

_____

> *Rebellion—I'm so over the obsession with looking*
> *good. I'm so over being good. You have to make a*
> *determination: Do you want to be good or do you*
> *want to be great?* —Eve Ensler

List a change that you have made for your family. Have you worked on controlling your temper? Did you relocate for a partner?

_____

_____

_____

_____

What have you done spiritually? Have you explored new ideas? Have you taught your children your beliefs? Have you put your values into action?

_____

_____

_____

_____

What have you done to improve your living space? Cleared clutter? Stopped moving every few years?

_____

_____

_____

_____

What is the most difficult thing you have done? What made it hard? What about you enabled you to do it anyway (courage, strength, trust, faith, sense of humor, intelligence, intuition)?

The hardest thing that I have done is

_____

_____

_____

_____

_____

_____

_____

> _He who knows others is wise._
> _He who knows himself is enlightened._ —Lao-tzu

> *We need to begin treating ourselves as well as we treat other people. That would be an enormous revolution.*
> —Gloria Steinem

What made it hard was

_____

_____

_____

_____

_____

What enabled me to do it anyway was

_____

_____

_____

_____

_____

> *If you have a blessing, the more you talk about it, the more you'll be blessed.* —Rev. Dr. Eloise Oliver

activity: mining for memories

Writing with your nondominant hand can unlock hidden memories or bring out unseen aspects of conscious memories. Lucia Capacchione writes of this technique in her book *Visioning*, "Through the non-dominant hand, the crystal-clear voice of truth speaks. Sometimes it sounds like a playful or emotional child. At other times ... it speaks words or ancient wisdom that sound like holy scripture. There is a sacredness and profound liveliness in these words from the uneducated and previously illiterate hand that has never been allowed to write" (2000, 39).

Take three of the exercises in this chapter that you were least interested in answering, or had the least to write about. Give yourself five minutes to write freely with your nondominant hand without rereading, censoring, or stopping. Just keep the pen moving. At first it will feel awkward and the writing will be messy. Do it anyway. This activity taps into a level of rich and authentic memories. What you write may not make sense at first. What you write may seem contradictory to what you previously remembered. Strong emotions may surface. Let yourself write. Allow new stories and images to be revealed. Do not correct yourself.

If you need additional space to write, use the blank lined pages at the end of this chapter to continue. The space below is unlined, because writing with the nondominant hand is messy and irregular at first. Write the exercise from the chapter that you will be using as you normally would, with your dominant hand. Check the clock, and write a new response with your nondominant hand for five minutes. Do this for each of the three exercises.

Exercise 1

_____

_____

_____

Exercise 2

_____

_____

_____

Exercise 3

_____

_____

_____

looking back

In this chapter you had an opportunity to look into your past while thinking about the nature of memory. You have had a chance to pull up the corners of what you assumed were realities to spy the exceptions underneath. In suspending all-or-nothing thinking, you opened to a view of your past that is gentler and a view of your self that is stronger. This is different from mere reexamination. Memory hinges on perception. You are getting used to flowing with this aliveness, accepting the necessity of peeking around corners to see what might also be true. As a more accurate sense of the past forms in your mind, varied and beautiful possibilities for your present awaken.

As you think, so shall you be. —William James

part
2

the realms

what's right with you in relationships

I don't associate with folks who don't prefer and freely choose exactly what I have to offer. I know that I have absolutely no time in my life for anyone to criticize any single part of me. I'm too busy, have too much to do, find it meaningless conversation. —Judi Hollis

correcting your vision

Perceiving yourself negatively in relationships can be a source of self-doubt and unnecessary suffering. If you are unhappy with your relationships—with partner, parents, or a friend—it often resounds internally as "If I were better in some way, I wouldn't have this problem" or "If this were a good marriage, we wouldn't struggle." Stepping back allows you to see that even the best relationships sometimes have difficulties. Furthermore, you are often blind to the high regard in which others hold you, even if challenges exist, such as competition between friends, a tendency to feel nagged by a partner, or

> *Reflection is the opposite of blame.* —Otto Scharmer

feeling like a parent does not approve of your life choices. Do you really know how much your friends love you? Do you feel how much family members respect you? This chapter offers an opportunity to look past the little things that trigger you and instead see what is essential and nourishing in these relationships. You can then actually receive the respect offered from the hearts of your loved ones.

Imagine what it would be like to live day by day if you allowed yourself the joy of knowing how much you are loved. Even if you argue with your friend frequently, she likely still admires you. The love that flows even from those with whom you may sometimes struggle is huge. Think of the confidence, peace, and sense of security that you would exude if you knew even half of the good thoughts that people have about you. For example, Liz and Ann are office buddies at a large advertising agency. Each woman is dynamic and bright, and they have been friends for two years. Liz found she was bickering with Ann more and more and feared their relationship was taking a familiar frustrating turn into blame and guilt. After reflecting, Liz was able to name not only three things she knew Ann saw and appreciated about her, she was able to remember how Ann's loyalty and humor were always there, too.

changing the rules

Historically, relationships were not necessarily a source of joy between conscious adults. They were often entered under great social pressure. Given their importance for mere survival, people had nothing to gain from questioning the health of a relationship. Nor did they have many tools to improve relationships. Today we are much more independent. We save for retirement, not expecting that our children will take us in when we can no longer care for ourselves. We are more likely to hire child care than to assume that relatives will provide it. Many people do not depend on spouses for financial survival.

But to enjoy life, we do need relationships—friends, people who feel like family, and often partners or spouses. Unlike in the past, most of us now have complete choice about who we spend time with. Yet when a relationship does not go as we would like, we experience angst: "Since we are both choosing to have this relationship, why are we having trouble?" The tendency is to think that you must be insufficient in some way: not thoughtful enough, cool enough, sexy enough, good enough at getting what you need, or lovable enough. You just know that you must be doing something wrong.

if it feels broke, don't fix it

Though most of us can learn to communicate better, there is no single flaw (or list of flaws) that you can fix and magically have a conflict-free life. In the absence of the clear roles and needs defined by more traditional relationships, today's friendships, familial relationships, and intimate relationships are formed in the messier territory of emotional needs. The contracts are not as clear in some ways, and though physical survival may not be an issue, the stakes may feel even higher. A lot of the uneasiness that you feel comes from being in unclear territory. You are learning how to navigate this extremely new world of at-will relationships. And you're a better navigator than you think. You need to give yourself credit. In this fast-paced, polyphonic, nonhomogenous, multiethnic, ever-changing culture, we are starting from scratch.

speaking the truth

Many people grew up burying dissatisfactions and hurts, saying "Oh, it's okay," when someone close hurt or neglected them. Never before have they had the opportunity and the challenge to communicate with utter honesty.

You need to be true to yourself to be functional. What does that look like? How do you get there? Sometimes you hit bumps in the road, and

> *Most childhood problems don't result from "bad" parenting, but are the inevitable result of the growing that parents and children do together.* —Fred Rogers

sometimes those bumps really hurt. This does not mean that you are bad or lacking. It means that you are a human being learning something new. You are sincerely trying to get close, know your needs, and genuinely connect with others.

Instead of assuming that a round of bickering indicates that your sister does not really respect you and that the relationship is flawed, you can try a different approach: "I know Amy loves me. She has said over and over that she loves spending time with me and she's so glad we are sisters. I appreciate the way she shows up for people she cares about. I know we can get this resolved." What if your sister feels closer to you than anyone in the world? How would it change your relationship and your life to know this and make it part of your reality?

the end of silence

As you journey toward wholeness, relationships get easier. In the last thirty years, amazing avenues for healing have come into being. Silence has been broken about many traumatic experiences. We now have the means and resources to heal from abuse and addictions of all kinds. We can get support to move past the legacy of a parent's alcoholism. Sponsors await to help us through our own 12-step programs. We have therapy, support groups, even online support to unbind us from the shame of sexual abuse. The stigma of diseases such as cancer has largely been lifted. More and more, we can talk about real issues, real challenges. This expanded range of acceptable expression in the broader culture also supports a more complete range of honesty between individuals.

As each person heals, relationship in general becomes easier and more fluid. True connection is no longer held hostage by unconscious reactions to unhealed emotional trauma that impede trust, deplete confidence, cause constant stress, and limit one's ability to be present. It is obvious: of course it is easier to be close to your brother once he has recovered from addiction to narcotics; of course it is easier to be in love with a woman who is no longer codependent.

What's in It for You

Although the tendency is to focus on the healing, what matters is where the healing gets you. The fruit of your labor toward wholeness is the joy in being alive. Self-acceptance is the key part of realizing that however we responded to past challenges and wherever that led us was perhaps part of a greater wisdom in ourselves. As we accept how we dealt with hurt or abuse, even if our only resource was to numb out with television, work, or drugs for a time, we can move into a place of deep self-appreciation for finding a way to survive. If we can accept ourselves at our "worst," we open to appreciating all that we are now.

Consciously and unconsciously, we all have made many good relationship decisions: we've created friendships, we've married, we've forgiven, we've separated. However arriving at these decisions may have felt at the time, you can now savor the self-love and self-preservation that enabled the often difficult work of choosing who you want in your life. As we get over our conditioning that makes it imperative to be nice, we see that expressing our wants and needs is an act of service to others. Asking for what we want is not the opposite of being nice. It makes us easier to get along with in relationships. It helps things go smoothly and averts drama.

The route through childhood is shaped by many forces,
and it differs for each of us. —Robert Wozniak

Allow yourself to reflect on the abundant territory of your own relationship history. Use these questions to celebrate the good in your relationships and to see clearly what you contribute to others.

What have you gained from a relationship struggle? Did it ever lead to a communication breakthrough or an "aha" moment?

_____

_____

_____

_____

Why do your friends like you? Name a few friends and list what you think they appreciate about you. What have friends written in your birthday cards, for example? Start a Medicine Bag file. Keep a folder of cards, letters, printed e-mail, and so on, in which others have praised you, expressed gratitude for your qualities, or just shared loving words. Open the file whenever you need its medicine.

_____

_____

_____

_____

> *The first step ... shall be to lose the way.* —Galway Kinnell

What good qualities do you have as a friend? List several.

_____

_____

_____

_____

With what friend or relative do you argue the most? Name a compliment that she or he has given you.

_____

_____

_____

_____

What has a parent or parent figure consistently praised you for? What is the most unexpected praise you have received from a parent or parent figure?

_____

_____

_____

_____

In what two ways are you a good sibling? Do you make time to talk with your brother or sister? Do you help your siblings laugh and blow off steam about family stresses?

_____

_____

_____

_____

In what ways are you a good child now? Do you call your parents regularly? Do you honor their memory?

_____

_____

_____

_____

_____

> *People used to say, "You're not married, what's wrong with you?" and I'd answer, "I'm not married, what's right with me!" —Pam Grier*

What values do you pass on to young people?

_____

_____

_____

_____

How did your partner compliment you when you first started dating? What does she or he value now?

_____

_____

_____

_____

What do you bring to romantic relationships? Are you great in bed? Do you encourage your partner to grow? Do you admit when you've made a mistake?

_____

_____

_____

_____

> *I need to take an emotional breath, step back, and remind myself who's actually in charge of my life.*
> —Judith M. Knowlton

Think of a person with whom you have ceased to communicate because he or she was not treating you well enough. What were you unwilling to live with? How did it feel to realize that you needed to end your relationship with this person?

I was unwilling to live with

_____

_____

_____

_____

_____

When I realized I needed to end my relationship with this person, I felt

_____

_____

_____

_____

_____

_____

> *Remembering the past gives power to the present.*
> —Fae Myenne Ng

With whom have you been generous, either with resources or with time? Write about what you have shared.

_____

_____

_____

_____

Who depends on you? For what? What do you provide for others?

_____

_____

_____

_____

_____ loves me even if I get fired from a job.

_____ loves me even if my body isn't the size that I want.

_____ loves me even if I get crabby sometimes.

_____ loves me even if I screw up.

activity: the a-list

Make a list of people you trust. Next to each person's name, note the positive qualities that she or he possesses. What do you admire about each person on your list? When you have completed your list, notice what kind of community you have built (caring, supportive, playful, familial, stimulating, etc.). Take a moment to credit yourself for creating a life that includes relationships with people of this caliber.

_____

_____

_____

_____

_____

_____

_____

Tell one person one reason you like them. Call, or write an e-mail or a letter. This doesn't need to be a big challenge. If you like, keep it light and simple: tell your friend that you love how she makes you laugh. If you want to elaborate on what you like or give more than one reason, go ahead and splurge.

No person is your friend who demands your silence or denies your right to grow. —Alice Walker

what you have gleaned

In this chapter you took inventory of what you provide to others, as well as what your loved ones believe about you. In listing those positives one after the next, a picture emerges that may be different from the one you previously held. A truer image emerges as you realize your value. When you see all that you provide for others simply by being who you are, you can dispense with the constant nagging sense that you are lacking or incomplete or that you never do enough for those around you. Lighten the demands you place on yourself to improve. Relax into the support you recalled in this chapter.

You also wrote about being encouraged, complimented, and even admired. You wrote about people you trust and what you admire about them. In these relationships, there is a seamless give-and-take. You give to those close to you by being who you are, and you benefit from the presence and personalities of those close to you. You each contribute and receive. When you recognize this, you see that you are finding your way in the unmapped territory of at-will relationships.

> *One loses many laughs by not laughing at oneself.*
> —Sara Jeanette Duncan

chapter five

celebrating your body

*No amount of self-improvement can make up
for a lack of self-acceptance.* —Unknown

the challenge is on

Body image is a challenging issue for many of us. We know that we are bombarded by unrealistic images and ideals, but despite our awareness, it's hard to reject what society feeds us. Even for a person who looks like a model, external criticism abounds. We need to be pioneers in this area. We need to say what is right about our bodies. With so few cultural forces insisting that we know and love our bodies, our faces, our hair, our hairlines, it is essential that we continuously give (or attempt to give) ourselves acceptance. The truth is, we are fine the way we are. We are fine when we wake up in the morning, we are fine despite the bad-hair day or the perceived extra twenty pounds. We deserve the pleasure and the inner peace that comes from being deeply comfortable in our own skins.

my assets, my self

If you have challenges around feeling confident in your appearance, you are not alone. In our culture, the challenge of self-acceptance is at a crisis level. It's not a coincidence, it's a bona fide marketing strategy. The diet industry takes in tens of billions of dollars each year. The cosmetic plastic surgery industry takes in over seven billion dollars annually. More younger women are going under the knife: 22 percent of those who undergo cosmetic procedures are between the ages of nineteen and thirty-four (ASAPS 2005).

In short, a lot of people are making a lot of money on dissatisfaction. Is it wrong to wear lipstick or color your hair? Of course not. What is wrong is having to suffer with the quiet but devastating feeling that you're not good enough. Since we have been trained to dislike at least some aspects of our looks from an early age, it is vital to create new mental habits. The first step is to have an awareness of our assets. Use the questions in this chapter to illuminate what is right about your body right now (not after the diet, exercise regimen, surgery, etc.). Every person can get to a place of increased peace and pride about their appearance.

a powerful practice

The process of change happens in everyday life. Have you ever shown up for a stress-management seminar or a yoga class and been told to quiet your mind? When this happens to us, we usually want to scream at the instructor. If it were that easy, we wouldn't be at the class! Unless we have a regular practice of quieting the mind, we cannot just turn off the racing thoughts at will. Self-acceptance is similar. We don't simply decide one day to stop

> *If anything is sacred, the human body is sacred.*
> —Walt Whitman

judging ourselves and love ourselves completely. Our brains do not let us. If it were that simple, we all would have made that choice years ago.

Focus Some Spare Moments on the Positive

There are so many negative messages about our appearance flying at us every day that we need to be in practice about self-love and self-acceptance. This does not mean that you need to expend a lot of time and effort meditating or saying affirmations in front of a mirror (although you might well enjoy and get benefit from doing these things). What will help you develop positive messages of your own is simple. First, respond to the questions in this chapter. This is the biggest and most important step, as it will require acknowledgment of the positive. Next, review the questions and responses frequently, adding new information or new detail. Then, when you have a moment at a red light or are waiting in line, take a minute to remember a compliment about your body or another positive statement from this chapter. If you like, put up notes to yourself in your home or on your steering wheel. Write just a few words in large print so that they are easy to read. For example, "I have great legs" or "Nick loves my smile." Savor these statements. They are true.

change for the better

The good news is that there are many more examples of ferocious self-acceptance than there were ten years ago. We have Camryn Mannheim showing the world that audiences want to see actresses of size on television. We have Pam Grier and Diane Keaton championing the beauty and sexiness

> *Even I don't look like Cindy Crawford in the morning.*
> —Cindy Crawford

> *The real voyage of discovery consists not in seeking new landscapes but in having new eyes.* —Marcel Proust

of being over fifty. In catalogs and advertisements we are finally seeing fabulous women with gray hair. There are reasons to be excited and hopeful. And through our delight and self-acceptance, we can open up possibilities for each other. Your work in this chapter will foster that sense of delight and possibility.

List a few times that your body has pleasantly surprised you. Can you bicycle farther than you ever imagined you could? Have you recovered from an illness more quickly than expected? Have you enjoyed a sexual breakthrough?

_____

_____

_____

_____

_____

_____

_____

Name a few of your health victories—major steps that you have made to take care of yourself. Have you quit smoking for any length of time? Started walking? Do you take actions to manage stress? Do you own an air filter or often eat organic food?

_____

_____

_____

_____

_____

_____

What lovely features do you share with your ancestors? Do you have your grandmother's cheeks or your father's hair color?

_____

_____

_____

_____

_____

> *We can make quiet but honest inventories*
> *of our strengths, since, in this connection, most of*
> *us are dishonest bookkeepers and need*
> *confirming "outside auditors."* —Neal Maxwell

> *A man cannot be comfortable without his own approval.*
> —Mark Twain

List at least three things that you like about your appearance.

_____

_____

_____

Name a few things that you do well regarding exercise. This can mean jogging three times a week or having the bravery to try new activities on and off throughout your life.

_____

_____

_____

List at least four compliments you have received about your physical self.

_____

_____

_____

What famous people share your features? For example, if you are short, list a few famous actresses, businesspeople, or politicians who are short. If you are lucky enough to have a prominent nose, you're in good company. Uma Thurman and Sara Jessica Parker have prominent noses, too. Do you have a knockout figure like Queen Latifah, or a sexy, irregular smile like Denzel Washington? If you don't know of any famous people who share your features, keep this question in the back of your mind for a few weeks. You will be surprised at what kind of information comes to you.

_____

_____

_____

_____

_____

Who has given you positive messages about your appearance throughout your life? Name two people and describe their praise.

_____

_____

_____

_____

_____

> *I want to sing like birds sing, not worrying who hears or what they think.* —Rumi

> *Only when you truly inhabit the body can you begin the healing journey.* —Gabrielle Roth

What do you like about your appearance that you would never tell anyone?

_____

_____

_____

_____

Stand in front of a mirror. Without thinking about it, what's the first thing that you see that you like? The second? The third?

_____

_____

_____

Find a picture of yourself that you love. This should be a picture of you looking great. If the situation that you were in when the picture was taken gives you mixed feelings, then cut the background out. For example, if the picture is with you and an ex, cut yourself or the ex out of the picture. Use a color photocopy if you like, if you don't want to cut the original. Look at the person in that picture. That beautiful person is you! Place the photo in your home where you can see it. If you can muster the courage, put it in a place of honor, such as the mantel or framed in your living room. What do you like about this picture?

_____

_____

_____

_____

Pick five of these features or aspects of you and describe in detail what you like about them.

- ☐ Your voice

- ☐ Your handshake

- ☐ Your tears

- ☐ Your yell

- ☐ Your walk

- ☐ Your dance

- ☐ Your self when you wake up in the morning

- ☐ Your laugh

- ☐ Your hug

- ☐ Your kiss

- ☐ _____

- ☐ _____

> *The most basic, fundamental tool of magic is the body.*
> —Vicki Noble

What if we smashed the mirrors and saw our true face?
—Elsa Gidlow

_____

_____

_____

_____

What is the last one you would pick? Write about that one in a
positive way.

_____

_____

_____

_____

In what ways are you physically strong?

_____

_____

_____

_____

> _Here in this body are the sacred rivers: here are the sun
> and moon as well as all the pilgrimage places. I have not
> encountered another temple as blissful as my own body._
> —Saraha

Think about three good friends. What do you like about them as people? Think of one or two things. Using that same type of kind attention, imagine that these friends are looking at you. They are noticing good qualities about parts of you that you have trouble liking. For example, you may not be able to say, "I like my stomach." However, a kind and honest friend would point out that your stomach is smooth and soft. Or, the kind friend might simply say, "Nice belly button."

Close your eyes. Pick a part of your body that you have trouble liking. What do the kind friends say?

_____

_____

_____

_____

_____

_____

Complete this sentence: If I felt totally comfortable with the way I looked

_____

_____

_____

_____

List three more things that you like about your appearance.

_____

_____

_____

activity: your superhero self

For this activity, you will fashion an image of yourself in which your personality strengths are expressed physically. If you were a superhero, what would your attributes be? What would you look like? What would your superpowers be? What would you be named? Would you have bulging muscles indicating your emotional resilience? Would you have long legs personifying extraordinary endurance or an ability to leap over obstacles? Maybe you have a magic cell phone that you use to make amazing ventures happen. Perhaps you would you have a picture of a lightbulb on your cape that depicts your incredible number of creative ideas. Maybe you have a glamorous, sexy outfit showing off your hips. Maybe you can make yourself invisible. Exaggerate your strengths. Make a positive, powerful caricature. Use the space on the next page to draw a picture of your superhero self. Or, collage together images that make up your superhero self. Describe her or him in detail on the lines below. Have fun. Nothing is too outrageous.

_____

_____

_____

_____

_____

_____

sizing up

By seeing who you really are physically, you have become more deeply aware and therefore more potent in all areas of your life. When you became a super hero, your self-image bloomed. You esteemed what is uniquely you. No other living body has the exact combination of strengths and experiences that yours has. Yes, that makes you valuable as a spouse, as a parent, as a coworker, and more. Most importantly, it makes you valuable as a human being. Now that you're better able trust your own value, you may find that asking for what you want is easier and that it is natural to expect respect. Saying yes and saying no to other people will be easier. Your own propensity for self-care will shift because you're seeing that you already are the prize that you have sought for years. Your body, your soul, is enough.

Finally, give yourself a huge pat on the back. It is extremely courageous to buck cultural conventions, even if those conventions are impossible to attain. Congratulations—you did it.

Listen. Make a way for yourself inside yourself. Stop looking in the other way of looking. —Rumi

your sexual self

Fear and guilt are the only enemies.
—Elisabeth Kübler Ross

To truly know and appreciate yourself, you must approve of and love your sexual self. In a sense, this is an extension of loving your body. But it is more than that. Sexuality emanates from your very core. Desire does not lie; your body wants what it wants. Regardless of how frequently you have sex or how confident you feel, you still need to recognize the good in your sexual self and your sexual history.

Although we may not have talked about it very much, we each have blazed our own sexual path. Its unfolding has been circuitous and has likely held surprises. We've taken risks, been swept away, flirted, survived, and befriended. We've bought condoms, had STD treatments, given birth, and felt embarrassed. Sexuality is a world within us. It deserves our attention as we reflect on the good we have done in caring for our sexual selves.

sexuality and human nature

To appreciate and honor who we are authentically, we need to recognize and carve away societal and media dictates of what our sexual selves should be. Sexual feelings are inherently human. It is human as well to sometimes have strong desires. Biologically, your primary directive is to procreate. Behind many urges and impulses is the drive to secure mating opportunities. This has enabled the human species to survive. We are each the end product of a sexual act. If you are taking an honest look at who you are, you have to include your sexual self.

Although the findings vary, surveys of sexual activity report that most adults have sex one to four times per week. But despite this general frequency, the reality that we are sexual is often refuted. We have to whisper to our confidants about it if we dare discuss it at all. There are real land mines to be avoided; mention sex at the wrong time and you could get fired, slapped, or sued. More typically, we hide from talking about sex because we fear shame and disgrace. You may have heard that the desire for sex is stronger than the desire for food. What would it be like to not be able to mention a food that you enjoy except to your closest friends?

Although much pornography is objectionable (if not simply a turnoff), the Internet industry tells us a lot about the strength of the human sex drive. The boom in use of the Internet was driven by porn. Internet technology was not developed and enhanced so that people could download e-mail faster and faster. The technology was developed at an astounding rate because of the extreme demand for viewing sex acts in high definition from the comfort of one's home. During the late 1990s, when coauthor Carolyn worked for a company that made software for building Web sites, the majority of customer calls came from Internet pornography businesses. The

> *It's hard to fight an enemy that has outposts in your head.*
> —Sally Kempton

100

company had not geared the product for that market, or solicited those customers in any way. Yet they were the customer base. (Interestingly, the customers calling with questions about creating Web sites were often women.) The experience of watching sex privately and anonymously on a personal computer was in such demand that, within a few short years, it drove the Internet industry to develop more quickly than anyone could have anticipated. Where does the combination of a strong sex drive and the requirement of silence about sex leave us? Isolated, ignorant, shamed, perpetually aroused?

it's a girl!

From birth, you are defined as a girl or a boy. It's the first thing that the doctor says when you are delivered. The first words you hear state your gender. From then on, there is enormous social pressure to behave as a typical female or male. Obviously, this demand can disrespect our true selves. At the same time, we get conflicting information about what is normal. Who dictates normalilty?

Ours is a culture hugely influenced by the media. We get many messages about how to behave and what is acceptable from the various media. Often, however, these media-driven messages may conflict with expectations placed on us by our family, religious tradition, or community. On one hand, women, particularly young and single women, are expected to be demure and chaste and not think of or desire sex. On the other hand, women are expected to be easily turned on and multiorgasmic. Thongs and push-up bras are being marketed to twelve-year-old girls. Men are expected to be superstuds, always on the make, mentally undressing every woman who

Maybe we do not have to be or perform perfectly.
—Julia Cameron

> *In looking for what is "right," we might have to accept parts of ourselves we formerly judged: our sexual longings, for instance. In our society, we just can't stand to say that women love sex.* —Judi Hollis

goes by. Yet if you seem too sexual at the wrong time, in the wrong place, with the wrong person, or at the wrong age, you are at best slutty—at worst filthy. And once people are over a certain age, their sexuality is represented nowhere in our culture. How frequently do you expect to have sex at the age of sixty-five? What is your emotional reaction to the idea of seniors feeling desire? It is still uncommon to see two people of different races in romantic relationships in movies and on television, and even now, heterosexuality is expected. The implication is that if you're not like a prescribed norm, there is something wrong with you. It's necessary to separate who we really are sexually from the image the media depict for us to emulate. You may not be able to change culture, but you can change how you respond to culture. How do you do this? The first step is self-knowledge.

know thyself

Each time you catch a glimpse of yourself in the mirror, find something attractive. Our brains are too comfortable seeing only the zit or the wrinkle. Instead of looking for "Beauty" with a capital B, notice what is appealing. If a person feels attractive, she or he will come across as sexy and attractive to others. A healthy twenty-five-year-old with lovely features, Deena never noticed admirers. Shy, though happy, she walked through life staring at the ground. She never considered herself good-looking enough to elicit a smile from a passer-by. One day she got a haircut not unlike the one she had worn for years. The hair cutter styled her hair into a simple yet stunning coif. Deena felt gorgeous, and her radiance was real. She saw two attractive young

> *A sound mind in a sound body is a short but full description of a happy state in this world.* —John Locke

men smile at her as she made her way home from the salon. Noticing the power of her internal shift, she recollected what made her feel attractive.

practicing optimism: what's right in this situation

We need to slow down and notice what's right about the moment: a scent, how light falls over your partner's hip, an exquisite sensation in just the right spot. It's easy to forget that sexuality is more than intercourse. It is also holding hands, playing footsie, giving a neck massage—any energetic contact between you and your partner. Spark. Some say that foreplay is everything that occurs between the times when you get naked: phone calls, daydreams, the way you interact with each other when picking up the dry cleaning. These varied energetic connections—thousands of moments of longing, security, and rapture—comprise your sensual self. As you develop a habit of seeing what is attractive about you and what is right in the moment with a partner, a healthy sense of security ripens. This is a great aphrodisiac (both for yourself and for a partner).

For many people, although physical features are attractive at first, what keeps their interest are deeper qualities. Trust is extremely important. People develop long-term intimacies with partners who don't manipulate or represent themselves falsely. Feeling safe is key.

Let yourself slow down as you respond to these questions. None of us have always known what we were doing, and all of us have made mistakes. Shame, or at least a little panicked embarrassment, is likely to come up as you mull your sexual past. Breathe, and keep writing. You will also be bouyed by the rediscovery of sureness and true connection.

> *Know thyself.* —Inscription at Delphi

In what ways have you grown sexually?

_____

_____

_____

_____

When have you asked for something sexually, even if you did not receive it? How did it feel to express your request?

_____

_____

_____

_____

Write about a positive sexual experience. It doesn't have to be with a partner or involve anything heavy, such as genital contact or an orgasm. Remember, there are fifteen blank sheets at the end of this book. Write as much as you like!

_____

_____

_____

_____

_____

What emotions did you feel? Bravery? Transcendental bliss? Shyness?

_____

_____

_____

_____

Write about a fantastic sexual experience that did involve genital contact or orgasm. How did you feel emotionally during it? What did you like about it—ease of interaction, sheer physical rapture, true intimacy, spontaneity? List as many aspects as you like. If there was a partner, what do you suspect he or she liked about the experience with you?

_____

_____

_____

_____

_____

_____

_____

_____

I want to do it because I want to do it. —Amelia Earhart

What do you like about your sensual self?

_____

_____

_____

_____

What are some good things that people have said about your sexual self? The words don't have to come from a lover.

_____

_____

_____

What do you find sexually attractive in a partner?

_____

_____

_____

_____

_____

> _Speak your mind—even if your voice shakes._
> —Maggie Kuhn

> *Power is strength and the ability to see yourself through your own eyes and not through the eyes of another.*
> —Lynn V. Andrews

What is the most surprising turn-on? Soft lips? A dazzling sense of humor? What does this illuminate about you?

_____

_____

_____

_____

List three compliments that you have given lovers.

_____

_____

_____

activity: savoring

Sit in a chair and close your eyes. Make sure you're comfortable, and know that there is nothing you must attend to for the next ten minutes. Feel your feet on the floor and sense how your chair is supporting you. Notice your breathing without trying to control it. Scan your body. What feels good right now? What feels relaxed? Take a minute and just savor pleasant bodily feelings. If you notice pain or tension anywhere in your body, do not try to do anything about it. Just let it be, and refocus your attention somewhere that feels loose and relaxed. Mentally scan your body, focusing on how each part feels. Start with your toes, then move to the arches of your feet, ankles, calves, and so on. Continue scanning upward, down your arms, up to the crown of your head. Does your left ankle feel different from the right one? What is the temperature of your hands? How tightly is your jaw hanging? Is there any area of your body that feels fluttery? Light? Buzzing? Let yourself feel what feels good.

reflections

In this chapter you dared to write about experiences that you may have never spoken about. In savoring the positive sexual experiences you've had, you replaced guilt with emotional gentleness. Extending such gentleness toward yourself is vital in an area of life where we are constantly being prodded to be different in some way—less inhibited, younger, more virile, and so on. Who you are sexually is just fine—your writing affirms that. After completing this chapter, you might notice yourself being re-inspired to connect, slow down, get out of your routine, or simply feel more at ease with who you are. Once silence is broken and the fact that you have a sexual side is not invisible, it becomes clear that sexuality is basic, common. It takes real bravery to think about your sexual history, let alone write about it. The work you did in this chapter has bolstered your mental and spiritual health.

> *Ever since there have been men, man has given himself over to too little joy. That alone, my brothers, is our original sin. I should believe only in a God who understood how to dance. —Henri Matisse*

discovering right work

Your work is to discover your work and then with all your heart to give yourself to it. —Buddha

Too many people are cut off from their innate gifts. Bored and numb, they go through the motions, working and coming home, looking forward only to the day when they can stop—ten, twenty, thirty years down the road. This is no way to live, and we do mean "live." In addition to spending half of our waking lives on the job, we spend hours each week preparing for work, talking about it when we're not there, and decompressing from its stresses. Since work takes up the hours of our lives, it's important that we like what we do, even love it, and get some value out of it for our bodies and souls. The more our work uses our unique talents and abilities, the closer we are to what has come to be called "right work."

right work: what is it?

Right work is the work that you do when you are using your gifts and unique abilities in a way that makes you glow with a sense of joy and meaning.

> *What can I do that isn't going to get done unless I do it,*
> *just because of who I am?* —Buckminster Fuller

Based on the Buddhist concept of right livelihood, right work is an expression of who you are. It is based on the idea that we each have a purpose, that we are intended to use our lives to make a contribution. You do not need to work for UNICEF to contribute to others. Creating sculpture is a useful contribution to society. Doing what you love can seem indulgent, but it is a service. For example, an artist must recognize that bringing more beauty into the world is of value. Our society needs art that stretches us and makes us think.

If you are currently doing your right work, congratulations! You truly are one of the lucky few. You will still benefit from using this chapter because it will help illuminate your strengths and contributions in the world of work.

Tess Daniel, a career coach in Portland, Oregon, believes that the biggest problem humanity faces right now is that most people are not doing their right work. In a conversation we had, she said, "This is a bigger problem than the nuclear threat," she says. "The problems that people were born to solve are not getting addressed. We have all of the talent needed to solve the world's problems right now." People need to know their talents and abilities and respect them by believing in them enough to use them.

How to Recognize Right Work

The clue to recognizing right work is that it is an activity you do because you love it. You are so present that you forget to look at the clock. The main marker of right work is that you lose a sense of time while doing it. Like a child playing, you are fascinated by what you are doing, and you are having fun. Another signal of right work is that you love doing it so much that you would do it without getting paid.

Although you will love doing your right work much of the time, you may not love it 100 percent of the time. Do not be thrown off. When you are learning a new skill that enables you to do your right work, it may feel hard or awkward. For example, if you have always worked as an employee but your right work involves starting a management consulting business, you will need to learn some accounting skills in order for your consulting business to thrive. Although accounting is not the focus of your work, and you may not enjoy bookkeeping, some knowledge of accounting is necessary. If your checks are bouncing and taxes are not getting paid, your time will be eaten up putting out accounting fires rather than doing the consulting work that you love. Or, there might be a skill directly related to the work tasks that you enjoy. If your passion is landscape gardening, you might find that designing watering systems is difficult at first. You might get anxious the first few times you approach a watering challenge that requires a complex system. However, this does not necessarily mean that landscape gardening isn't for you. You simply need time to develop ease and confidence with the task. In either case, when you have the skills and use them, you delight in what you're doing overall.

hinderances

Two main forces keep us from knowing and doing our right work. One is external—economics—and the other is internal: feeling you don't deserve satisfying work.

Who'll Pay the Rent?

According to coach Tess Daniel, economics is the chief force that works against knowing and doing your right work. The most common roadblock to

> *I am not a businessman, I am an artist.* —Warren Buffet

> *Reminding one another of the dream that each of us aspires to may be enough for us to set each other free.*
> —Antoine de Saint-Exupéry

right work is the thought, "I don't know how I'll make a living doing this." There is so much pressure to make a living that discovering your unique contribution to the world can easily get put off, year after frustrating year. Midlife crises often come from the realization that you are not doing what you're here to do. Men especially often feel so much urgency to provide that they don't see the option of considering right work, while women are socialized to believe that their contribution is to support others.

Our educational system can be a further hinderance in finding right work. Instead of fostering and nurturing talents, the system tends to support weaknesses. For example, a student who struggles with math gets extra help in the subject and is expected to spend extra time and attention on it. At the same time, what is easy and comes naturally to a student is often taken for granted. The area in which a student excels often indicates an innate talent that could be expressed later in life as right work. Gifts, as well as problematic areas, need to be developed with extra time and attention.

What if You Loved It?

Another major obstacle is not feeling deserving of enjoyable work. Many people possess limiting beliefs that are unconscious: work is work; work is drudgery; work is how you pay the bills. To feel deserving of right work, you need to believe that your essence is worth developing, nurturing, and investing in. It requires strong self-esteem to believe that you have something worth expressing and that you can make a contribution that is of value to others. When well-meaning parents do not see how a child's talents will lead to a career, they discourage the development of those talents. These parents don't know that right work, whatever it may be, supports financial stability. Children raised this way grow up investing time and resources in training that they hope will make money, all the while neglecting the development of natural skills and talents. But this state of affairs can seem perfectly natural in families where everyone is expected to quash their natural talents in order to pursue more "practical" goals. And, after all, if other family members settled for less, many children wonder why they should deserve to do what they really want.

Who saw their parents really happy, loving the work that they were doing? Growing up, did you look forward to working as an adult? Did you think, "One day, I'll get to do what I really like and get paid well for it. My job will be great." Even those who enjoy their jobs rarely share that enjoyment with others. Somehow, the norm is to complain about what's wrong, even if you are pretty happy with your current work life. Why is this? At least in part, it's because we don't feel we deserve to be happy. People wrestle with a sense of deserving to exist, let alone enjoy their work. When we were children, we may not have seen that enjoyment modeled by the adults in our lives. Or, it might seem indulgent to get paid for something that is pleasurable. Someone has to design sports cars; why not you? Someone has to be a professional wine taster. Someone has to work with autistic children. Luckily, what each of us truly wants is different, and there is plenty of opportunity to go around. Because you secretly want to open a restaurant, it might seem that many people harbor the same desire. Then the anxious thinking takes over, "Everyone can't open a restaurant. If I did, mine would never make it. Why bother?" In actuality, the world needs what you have, whether you are a brain surgeon, a revolutionary, or a poet.

You Are Meant to Like Your Work

There are all kinds of ways that your brain chatters to keep you from believing that work should be enjoyable. After all, if you relished your work, a huge chunk of your life would be enjoyable. Is that really what you expect? Can you envision that for yourself? Or is suffering familiar? If so, you're not

> *If you make believe that ten guys in pin-striped suits are back in kindergarten class playing with blocks, you'll get a rough picture of what life in a corporation is like.*
> —Lee Iacocca

alone. But you can successfully challenge the notion that work should be hard and life is a struggle. Life can be different. Work can be wonderful. It has to be: your soul won't rest until your life is where it is meant to be. That is why you are working on yourself, why you were drawn to this book.

Everyone who works wants to love their job. You want to show up in the morning glad to be there, greet the people you see each day, and be engaged in what you do. Each of us are meant to be doing our right work, work that we love, for good pay, and in a constructive environment. Work is meant to be a puzzle piece whose odd bulges and irregular curves fit just right into our lives.

Once you feel deserving, pursuing your goals doesn't feel like a herculean effort. Whether going after a promotion or starting down a new path, it won't seem so intimidating when you know that you can excel at the required tasks. The key to moving closer to right work is awareness of your abilities—your talents and what you are capable of learning and enduring on the job. The truth is that everyone who ever hired or promoted you did so for a reason, and it was not sympathy. They thought that your unique presence on the job would make them look good and help them either make money or achieve their goals.

figuring it out

So how do you figure out what your right work is? Tess Daniel emphasizes that on some level, each person really does know what it is that he or she is meant to do. There is a simple exercise that helps bring this self-knowledge up through the fear and limiting beliefs into consciousness: Make a declaration. Say out loud, "I now know what my right work is." Then each day, meditate, walk, or journal, keeping that declaration in mind. It may take a day, it may take a year, but you will get the message. This technique is tried and true. If it appeals to you, phrase the declaration as a prayer: "Dear Spirit, may I now know what my right work is." Though it requires some effort to determine your right work, it is worth it. For many people, right work is so obvious that they don't see it. Their right work is something that they do naturally, and this contradicts the common belief that work has to be something they dislike. As you can see, the idea of right work really goes against the grain.

Getting from Here to There

There are a few strategies for transitioning into doing your right work. So that you can pay the rent and feed your kids, a plan that works for most people is to get a job that doesn't drain all of your energy. Relieving immediate financial pressure will give you the mental space you need to explore; having a stable base, you can begin doing your right work on the side. After all, how effective will you be at developing your tap-dancing business or becoming a motivational speaker if you are stressed to the max every time a bill is due? You may have to humble yourself. Your "in the meantime" stable job may be unglamorous. You might have to forgo a job with an impressive title so you can forgo a sixty-hour workweek. But think of how wonderful it will be to do what you love even some of the time, knowing that you are on a path toward doing work that you love full-time.

Keep in mind that your right work must provide something to others. Remember, a dance performance that inspires its audience is providing

> *Most do violence to their natural aptitude, and thus attain superiority in nothing.* —Baltasar Gracian

> *You are not here merely to make a living. You are here to enable the world to live more amply, with greater vision, and with a finer spirit of home and achievement. You are here to enrich the world. You impoverish yourself if you forget this errand.* —Woodrow Wilson

something. Although professional mountain climbers sometimes get sponsorships and endorsement deals, most people won't get paid to climb a mountain no matter how much they love it. A person can get paid to teach others how to climb a mountain, however, or write a book about the adventure.

Another strategy, which may be employed at the same time, is metaphorically called "walking through the next door." You have to go through whatever door is open to walk through. Once inside, you will recognize what comes next. You've got to pursue what calls you, even if it doesn't seem to make sense. For example, David wanted to become a psychiatrist, but had a laundry list of reasons why he couldn't. An intelligent thirty-two-year-old man, he held a series of unsatisfying jobs. He would start each new position with great excitement but would be bored in six months. Then he'd spend the next few years feeling miserable at work, only to take a new job with the expectation that this one would finally make him feel alive and engaged. Ten years into that cycle, he was ready for change. Since his teen years, David had been drawn to psychiatry, but the costly and lengthy educational investment seemed intimidating. Although his wife supported his dream, he felt that student loans would be too burdensome. What if the family needed to buy a new car? Wasn't it self-indulgent to take on five years of schooling at the age of thirty-two? Shouldn't he and his wife be buying a house like so many of their friends? David argued and argued with himself, refusing to take action toward his goal. Instead, what immediately called him was playing guitar. So, he walked through that door. For six months he played guitar as much as possible in local bars and coffeehouses. Then, almost without realizing that he was doing it, he began applying to psychiatry programs. By pursuing what called him, regardless of how rational or practical it seemed, David set off on a path. The path is rarely linear, but will lead to the right place. Take the next step. Right work is rarely achieved in one giant leap.

getting off your "buts"

For many years coauthor Carolyn thought that having creative work was an impossibility. With all the diverse work opportunities in the San Francisco Bay Area, she was convinced that she needed to have a traditional job, sit in a cubicle each day, and work for a corporation. Although she enjoyed aspects of these jobs, such as fantastic coworkers and an exciting work pace, she knew that to be satisfied on a deeper level she needed something else. Obstacles bubbled up in her head: "But what would it pay? Am I talented enough? The field that I am interested in is so competitive, and I don't have formal training." The "buts" went on and on. Looking back, she sees that the main sticking point was she didn't believe that she deserved to have work that she liked. It contradicted her Puritan work ethic. Work needed to have misery in it in order to count. Her brain was insistent on the necessity of the obstacles, but her soul was not convinced. She was not capable of remaining unfulfilled, so she worked with a career counselor and began a journey of figuring out what excited her. The path was nonlinear and took a few years, but led her to greater self-knowledge. Before she could use her strengths and talents, she had to be able to see them.

Coming from a family of kind and caring people, Carolyn grew up with the idea that the best work that she could do would be directly helping

> *God gives each of us special talents and gifts. It is both*
> *our privilege and our duty to make the most of them.*
> —Robert E. Allen

others—feeding the starving, curing disease, and, yes, even saving whales. Now she realizes that whatever one provides through expression of right work, be it house painting or personal training, supports people who do devote their lives to service. We all have a role.

change as the norm

During the last twenty years, our culture has been increasingly challenged with changes to the work world such as outsourcing, layoffs, and the shift toward retaining contractors instead of hiring in-house employees. Flexibility has been forced on us. The silver lining of decreasing job security is the opportunity to go after what you want. You can make changes to your path: people now expect to change jobs, if not careers, several times during their work lives. You can leave a job without shame or guilt. The benefit to this new landscape is the opportunity to search for what you want until you find it. Furthermore, changing careers does not seem impossible when you recall the other major transitions that you have engineered in your life.

Change happens fluidly when you let yourself know what you want. Completing the exercises in this chapter (as well as others), will help you to know better what you enjoy, what you're drawn to, and what you have excelled at time and time again. The exercises will illuminate your right work. Change may feel daunting or downright scary; however, in the end, staying stuck is more difficult than making change. Ultimately, what causes misery is staying in a situation that does not reflect who you really are or give you what you really want. Whether you're interested in making a job change or simply want to feel more enthusiasm for your current job, completing this chapter will help.

Before you begin, remember when listing your experiences to be sure to include work that you have done for organizations other than formal employers. For example, include volunteer work, contributions you make to your children's clubs, as well as activities like gardening or art that you would usually consider hobbies.

During what activities do you lose track of time?

_____

_____

_____

_____

What is the most fun you have had at work?

_____

_____

_____

_____

What skills or abilities have you discovered on the job? This can be in a current job or in a previous one. Did you discover an ability to lead people? Realize that you are exceptionally patient? Are you better with numbers than you had ever imagined?

_____

_____

_____

_____

_____

> *I don't like work—no man does—but I like what is in work: the chance to find yourself.* —Joseph Conrad

Specifically, how do you use your talents at work, either in past jobs or at your current job?

_____

_____

_____

_____

_____

_____

What makes you a good employee, coworker, or supervisor?

_____

_____

_____

_____

What do you enjoy most about your current job? The day-to-day tasks? The opportunity to write reports? The pay and the lifestyle it affords? The effect on the lives of others?

_____

_____

_____

_____

_____

Another powerful tool for unlocking right work is asking a few people who know you well what you are good at. What do they say? Resist the urge to be modest!

_____

_____

_____

_____

_____

_____

_____

To feel valued, to know, even if only once in awhile, that you can do a job well is an absolutely marvelous feeling.
—Barbara Walters

Complete this sentence and elaborate on it: At past jobs, coworkers remember me for

_____

_____

_____

_____

_____

Recall some praise that you have been given at work about your performance. Include offhand comments as well as formal reviews.

_____

_____

_____

_____

_____

_____

The better you listen to the voice within you, the better you will hear what is sounding outside. And only she who listens can speak. —Dag Hammarskjöld

activity: the real resume—part I

On the lines below, you will be exploring the skills and experience that you've gained in past and current jobs. The experiences usually listed on a traditional resume will be left out. Instead, this one will include the real-world skills that have enabled your success. At what point did you learn to negotiate a good salary? Which situation made you more shrewd? Which job taught you how to deal with a difficult boss? These skills are as valuable as technical job skills. The Real Resume documents the grit it can take to reach your goals. It shows you what you're made of. You deserve credit for meeting these kinds of challenges. It was work—hard work. Noticing how you met challenges (in any area of life) provides indicators for right work. This activity is as powerful as it is satisfying. To start with, a few questions are provided. Once you get the idea, make up some Real Resume items of your own.

At what point did you learn to negotiate a good salary?

_____

_____

_____

_____

_____

_____

_____

Which job taught you how to deal with a difficult boss?

_____

_____

_____

_____

_____

_____

_____

Your Real Resume questions:

_____

_____

_____

_____

_____

You've got to find the force inside you. —Joseph Campbell

> *The most fundamental assumption of the underground managerial world is that truth is a good idea when it is not embarrassing or threatening—the very conditions under which the truth is especially needed.* —Chris Argyris

activity: the real resume—part II

In the next exercise you will look at how these skills might relate to a job of your dreams. How have you met challenges? How would you like to apply your shrewdness, tenacity, or assertiveness? If you're good at defending and promoting your own ideas, where might that skill take you? What might being able to defend your ideas allow you to do? If prior challenges incited you to begin networking, how could that skill serve you in your dream job? You are not expected to immediately know what your right work is. For the purposes of this exercise, pick an occupation that sounds like fun, even if it seems impractical (for instance, it requires moving to China, you have no prior experience in the field, or you can't imagine how you would make money doing it). You are not committed to pursuing or even investigating this type of work. What career would be fun for you? Coaching athletes? Piloting airplanes? Pediatrics? Pick two. You will use one at a time to complete the following exercise.

Fantasy job: _____

Skill from Real Resume: _____

_____

_____

_____

Skill from Real Resume: _____

_____

_____

_____

Skill from Real Resume: _____

_____

_____

_____

Skill from Real Resume: _____

_____

_____

_____

Fantasy job: _____

Skill from Real Resume: _____

_____

_____

_____

Skill from Real Resume: _____

_____

_____

_____

Skill from Real Resume: _____

_____

_____

_____

Skill from Real Resume: _____

_____

_____

_____

a pat on the back

Good work! In this chapter you recollected what you enjoy doing as well as what you've been recognized for on the job. You have been bolstered by the sense of accomplishment that comes from seeing just how much you've done well and heartened by glimmerings of what work quickens your spirit. The first part of the Real Resume provided great self-acknowledgment and satisfaction. The second part empowered you by revealing that you are already part of the way across the bridge of transition.

The path to right work is not linear. The writing you've done in this chapter supports you circling in toward your unique expression and contribution. By holding these newly uncovered memories and strengths in your mind, the next step on your path will become clear. Keep reviewing what you have written. Write more as you discover more about yourself. This will keep the doors opening and enable fluid next steps—and there will be many. Few people discover and commit to their right work all at once. Trust that the process is unfolding at the right pace. Commit to a single, doable next step, such as journaling or meeting with a career counselor. As strengths and gifts are already within you, so is their expression—right work. Supported by vast self-knowledge acquired on these pages, you are ready to let your true expression emerge.

> *Your health is bound to be affected if, day after day, you say the opposite of what you feel, if you grovel before what you dislike and rejoice at what brings you nothing but misfortune. Our nervous system isn't just a fiction; it's a part of our physical body, and our soul exists in space, and is inside us, like the teeth in our mouth. It can't be violated forever with impunity. —Boris Pasternak*

part
3

putting it all together

chapter eight

creating your own affirmations

An affirmation is a strong, positive statement that something is already so. —Shakti Gawain

just the facts

Each person has the power to change her or his self-talk using affirmations. If you want to feel more confident at work, the standard approach that you may have heard is to say the affirmation "I feel confident at work," nothing more. The method in this book is more personalized, tailored exactly to fit your needs so it can be more effective.

The exercises that you have already completed in this book reveal the good that you have done, said, and experienced. Use that knowledge as a basis for change. In this book, a woman looking to feel increased confidence in her job is asked to write specifically about what she does well at work, compliments given to her by her coworkers, skills, good ideas that she has had at work, and what she contributes to the organization. As you know, these things are facts. She can then look at the evidence, reading a fact such as "My superiors have always told me that I have exceptional people skills," and feel its truth. Looking at ten actual reasons why one should feel confident at work adds tremendous power to the chosen affirmation, "I feel confident at work."

In this chapter, you will learn to create personal affirmations based on the writing you have done in previous chapters. What do you want more of in your life? More joy? One way to create more joy is to notice what joy already exists, surrounding you. It is powerful to bring to light the immense positive aspects of your current life, as you have done in earlier chapters through your writing and recollecting. Going forward, personal affirmations are a powerful tool to augment and magnify this work.

getting used to it

Even the most cynical among us have benefitted from using affirmations. Scott Adams used them to create the *Dilbert* comic strip when he wrote the statement "I write the number-one comic strip in America" over and over. The result was a sarcastic comic about corporate America that millions of people could relate to. Affirmations don't have to be sugary. They do not make the user starry-eyed or simple. They are a tool to help you get what you want out of life. Period.

Affirmations are easy to do. What is difficult is ignoring the nagging, negative voice that comes up when we first start them. It's the one that says, "I feel silly. This is stupid." Even though we are hungry for the benefit of the affirmation, beginning may be difficult. At first, saying our chosen affirmation over and over may feel uncomfortable, fake, or awkward. Recall that learning to drive felt awkward, too. But you wanted the benefits of being able to drive, so you stuck with it. As you practiced over and over, you never questioned that your repetitive actions would lead to the desired result: the ability to drive a car. Affirmations work the same way. Use one consistently and it becomes reality. Like practicing your driving, done consistently and correctly, affirmations are guaranteed to work.

The challenge is not getting affirmations to work; the challenge is getting used to affirmations. Everyone thinks that "doing affirmations" is a little hokey at first. Everyone feels shy about it. Try it anyway. See how powerful your words can be. If you are new to affirmations, be patient. Do not contemplate whether or not the process will work or how long it will take. Although you do not need to believe that it will work to get the desired benefit, doubting may sap your motivation. Safeguard your motivation because repetition of affirmations is key.

What do you do if you're using an affirmation about success and the thought "I will never succeed" goes through your mind? Let that thought go. One contradictory thought will not undo the growth you are gaining through use of an affirmation. Don't worry about it! If you keep working your affirmation, your affirmation will keep working.

true or false?

We all have self-talk—repetitive messages that play in our brains, sometimes consciously, sometimes not. It's like a tape playing over and over, telling us who we are: "I can be a nurse, but I can never make it as a painter" or "I will have an anxiety attack if I board an airplane." The brain does not know what is factual and what isn't. It has been taught all kinds of limitations, true or not, and it informs your life reflecting these beliefs. Affirmations declare a new reality. Say the same words often enough, and the brain will believe them.

how to create an affirmation

When creating your affirmations, there are a few guidelines to keep in mind that will maximize the potency of your statements. Choose words that are natural for you. For example, which word would you choose to complete the phrase "I now have a loving ... [partner, spouse, husband, girlfriend, or sweetheart]"? Edit the affirmation until it feels right. Rearrange the words or use different words until the affirmation resonates with you. Make short statements—they are often the most powerful. Even though you're creating a situation that has yet to be, make sure that affirmations are in the present tense. Avoid saying "I will" or "I am becoming." Instead, say "I am" or "I now have."

Step by Step

Let's say that Joanna wants to have more money. Currently, she has a relatively well-paying job, but her New York City rent is high. She has found it difficult to keep any savings. She berates herself for perpetually carrying a few thousand dollars in credit-card debt. She chose to base an affirmation on responses to the question "What good financial decisions have you made?" Joanna wrote:

1. I always pay my rent on time.

2. When I owed on my taxes a few years back, I worked out a payment plan with the IRS and stuck to it.

3. I take advantage of my company's 401k matching plan.

4. I am keeping myself afloat in a financially challenging city.

5. I have eight weeks of paid sick time saved in case of emergency.

In pausing to examine her responses, Joanna saw how consistent she was with making expected payments. She also had the foresight to save some sick time in case of illness or injury and to plan for retirement by taking advantage of her company's 401k plan. Beyond that, she saw that she was a survivor, with the grit and gumption to forge a life for herself in a place where life is expensive. Based on her new insights, she created the

136

affirmation "I am strong and good with money." After using this affirmation for one month, she chose, "I have a solid savings." Almost without realizing it, she began paying down her credit-card bill. Within six months, she was debt free and had a modest savings. She was able to break her old habit of spending any extra money immediately and left her savings untouched.

Now it's your turn to try creating an affirmation.

What I want in my life is _____

Are there any questions from previous chapters that relate to what you want?

_____

_____

_____

_____

_____

List some examples of when you've had this or something like this, bringing in any memories that come into play from exercises in previous chapters.

_____

_____

_____

_____

_____

_____

In contemplating my responses, I recognize that _____

_____

_____

_____

_____

Brainstorm some ideas for an affirmation that will capture the essence of your insight. Play around with the wording until it feels right.

_____

_____

_____

_____

_____

_____

_____

_____

My affirmation is _____

_____

A few more templates are provided below. You do not need to complete them all right now.

What I want in my life is _____

Are there any questions from previous chapters that relate to what you want?

_____

_____

_____

_____

List some examples of when you've had this or something like this, bringing in any memories that come into play from exercises in previous chapters.

_____

_____

_____

_____

_____

In contemplating my responses, I recognize that _____

_____

_____

_____

_____

Brainstorm some ideas for an affirmation that will capture the essence of your insight. Play around with the wording until it feels right.

_____

_____

_____

_____

_____

_____

_____

My affirmation is _____

_____

What I want in my life is _____

Are there any questions from previous chapters that relate to what you want?

_____

_____

_____

_____

_____

List some examples of when you've had this or something like this, bringing in any memories that come into play from exercises in previous chapters.

_____

_____

_____

_____

_____

_____

In contemplating my responses, I recognize that _____

_____

_____

_____

_____

_____

Brainstorm some ideas for an affirmation that will capture the
essence of your insight. Play around with the wording until it feels
right.

_____

_____

_____

_____

_____

_____

_____

_____

My affirmation is _____

_____

As you might imagine, the more you do this, the easier it is. The key is
to spend as much time on each step as is needed. If the words or ideas don't
come to you quickly, try not to get anxious. Stay in a playful brainstorming
mind-set. Nothing is set in stone. You can change and recraft at any time.

using your affirmation

There are several effective techniques for using an affirmation. Pick one, or combine them.

1. Once a day, say your statement out loud ten times with confidence and energy.

2. Write the affirmation on several sticky notes and place them where you will see them often throughout the day: on the bathroom mirror, on the steering wheel of your car, on a cabinet door, on the side of your computer monitor, and so on. Do what is needed to maintain a comfortable level of privacy.

3. Write the affirmation on a sheet of paper twenty times each day, saying the words to yourself as you write. You will be surprised how little time this takes.

4. While you are taking a shower, doing dishes, or walking to the bus stop, repeat your affirmation inwardly.

Experiment with different techniques. To see clear results in the smallest amount of time, work with one affirmation at a time. Avoid spreading your intentions too thinly. Work with it each day for thirty days. Choose a new affirmation to work with as you feel ready.

activity: a quick fix

Deep breathing is an easy technique that allows you to relax and focus. Use this process for calming and stillness if you feel anxious about responding to a question or completing an activity in this book, or whenever you're feeling stressed and vulnerable. It only takes a few minutes to do, and the reward is immediate.

As you breathe out, carbon dioxide is released, and as you breathe in, oxygen flows into your lungs. As the body circulates oxygen to your brain, you think more clearly. Your body feels more relaxed and less fatigued. Breathing deeply for five minutes is helpful. You may do it as many times a day as is useful to you. The longer you practice this technique over time, the more benefits you will notice.

Here is a step-by-step guide. Read it through first before you try it. Begin practice for one minute and work up to five minutes over a week's time.

1. Sit in a comfortable chair with your back straight, feet flat on the floor, and your arms supported by a chair or pillow.

2. Close your eyes if you like, or focus your eyes on a distant, stable object.

3. Breathe in through your nose while expanding your diaphragm muscle out. This is the muscle just below your chest and above your waist. If you like, place one hand on that area. Feel your hand move out as you breathe in and move in as you breathe out.

4. As you breathe in, count "One, two, three" to yourself, then pause for a moment.

5. Breathe out through your mouth and notice your diaphragm going in toward the rest of your body.

6. Begin to count and breathe again.

7. Continue these repetitions for five minutes.

8. Say to yourself, "I feel refreshed, relaxed, and in control."

Although there is an immediate benefit to deep breathing, there are longer-term benefits as well. Some people who practice this technique begin to notice they begin to feel an elevation in overall mood in about one week. This technique cannot harm you. If you overbreathe/hyperventilate, a monitor in the base of your brain will take over and restore a less rigorous breathing pace that will correct the oxygen–carbon dioxide balance in your body. Some people report that they feel a little light-headed or that they notice feeling tingling in their hands. If you don't like that feeling, just breathe less deeply for thirty to sixty seconds. As you become more and more relaxed after several weeks of practice, be sure to stretch all your muscles when you're done with each session and stand up slowly since your blood flow has temporarily changed somewhat.

An extra benefit may be derived by practicing this breathing when you are in bed and ready to sleep. This kind of breathing helps you get more restful, restorative sleep—at least in the early part of the sleep cycle.

Sometimes people like to make their own cassette tapes of the exercise. This has an added benefit because you are instructing yourself and taking charge of your body. Just remember as you make your tape to go slowly and try to fit your breathing pattern to the tape. If your mind wanders at any time, you can just refocus your attention to the movement of your diaphragm and your number count or you can write down the intruding thought (if it is extremely important to remember) and then go back to your deep breathing practice.

Have fun. Become skilled. You will be rewarded for your efforts!

Now that you are a savvy excavator of positive facts, you've used this chapter to shift gears, creating questions that prompt recollection. This required entering new cognitive territory and learning new skills. Kudos on challenging yourself yet again.

As you developed facility with writing affirmations, you received one of the key benefits of using this book. Creating affirmations in your own voice, reflecting your experience, is the tool that allows you to bridge past experiences to the future that you want for yourself. By using your own individualized affirmations, you keep the newly discovered truth in mind. This is vital. In our culture we rebury the positive as quickly as it is brought to light.

Give these new processes a chance, even if they feel awkward at first or if it takes a little time to feel the desired effects. Trust that you're doing it right. Trust that you are worth the effort.

chapter nine

writing your own inquiry exercises

Nothing unless first a dream. —Carl Sandberg

In addition to writing personalized affirmations, you can create your own Inquiry Exercises to help address a particular challenge. Inquiry Exercises are simply questions and directives like those used throughout this book ("List two ways that you are a good parent") that you create yourself. Although the questions and directives in previous chapters include issues common to many of us, each person's life contains unique challenges. This book could not possibly include enough exercises to address the infinite issues that one might face. In this chapter you will learn how create Inquiry Exercises that are tailored to meet your specific need, such as when you are:

- Desiring increased mental peace

- Working through a relationship issue (like wanting to argue less or connect more deeply)

- Wanting to feel happier and less depressed

- Feeling lonely

- Ill and afraid

- Wanting to save more money

- Wanting to feel more connected to your spiritual tradition

- Trying to eliminate a phobia, or

- Wanting to feel more confident in any situation or area of life.

Creating tailored Inquiry Exercises allows you to apply the process described in this book to any challenge that arises in your life. With this tool at your disposal, you will be able to surmount obstacles with speed and agility.

Just after Angelo sold his first screenplay, he went through weeks of self-doubt as a writer. His enthusiasm had carried him so far: he'd spent the prior two years writing the first draft and crafting a hefty, detailed proposal to secure a movie deal. Tirelessly, he'd pitched his screenplay over and over. But when the project got the green light, he got nervous. All of a sudden he had six weeks to turn the screenplay draft into a polished script. Using the techniques in this chapter, he wrote questions to woo back his confidence. That was his goal. Then, after he brainstormed a few key words, he wrote the following questions:

- When have I received praise for my writing? What was said?

- What are my other creative successes?

- What are my favorite things about this screenplay?

- When have I risen to professional challenges in the past?

He answered those questions in detail and reviewed the answers whenever he heard the spooky sound of self-doubt in his head. In a matter of days he was back on track, enthusiastic, confident, and productive.

getting started

First an example is provided, then we will build sample Inquiry Exercises together, creating the situations you want in your life. The exercise is a four-step process: clarifying your goal, brainstorming key words, building the inquiry exercises yourself, and then answering the questions you've written.

Let's start with an example closely linked with ideas from chapter 5, "Celebrating Your Body." If you'e feeling chronically frumpy, try writing an inquiry exercise to affirm your appeal.

1. The first step is clarifying the goal. In this case, the goal is "feeling attractive."

2. Write a goal statement. Keep it simple. In this case it could be "I feel attractive, sexy, and confident."

3. Start by brainstorming words for your Inquiry Exercise. Imagine what you are looking for, or think of the opposite of what you want to change. In this example, perhaps words like "confident," "gorgeous," "diva," and "appeal" come to mind. The words you brainstorm will spur your thinking. Write them down.

4. What questions might help you consider yourself worthy of reaching your goal? What questions help you recall a history of having had the quality you seek or something like it? Have you received any compliments in this area? Or, when else have you been able to create a desired quality or situation—a job, a friendship, an opportunity, healing? For example you might ask, "In the past, when have I felt hot? Who has told me that I am attractive, sexy, or pretty? What exactly did she or he say? What was the circumstance?"

5. The final step is to answer the questions you've created.

Let's try another example. Perhaps you want to increase your income.

Start by clarifying the goal. Write a goal statement.

_____

_____

What words come to mind when you think about increased income?

_____

_____

_____

To fully know that you deserve greater financial ease, what questions could you ask yourself? For instance, "What good money decisions have I made? When have I felt worthy of a good income?"

Write down a few pertinent questions that resonate for you. The rules that apply when responding to exercises in prior chapters apply here: don't hold back, resist the urge to censor yourself, and keep your pen moving.

_____

_____

_____

_____

_____

_____

Now answer these questions.

_____

_____

_____

_____

_____

_____

_____

_____

_____

_____

_____

With your new understanding about how the process works, tailor some Inquiry Exercises to a goal of your own.

Think of something that you want, large or small.

What I want is _____

Write a goal.

_____

Brainstorm some words that reflect or signify that desired situation.

_____

_____

_____

_____

_____

_____

Now brainstorm some ideas for questions. Some starters are provided.

When have I experienced this in the past? If I haven't experienced this exact thing, when have I experienced something similar?

_____

_____

_____

_____

_____

_____

_____

_____

_____

_____

Answer your questions.

_____

_____

_____

_____

_____

_____

_____

_____

_____

_____

_____

Try another.

What I want is _____

Write a goal.

_____

Brainstorm some words that reflect or signify that desired situation.

_____

_____

_____

_____

_____

_____

_____

Now brainstorm some ideas for questions. Some starters are provided.

When have I experienced this in the past? If I haven't experienced this exact thing, when have I experienced something similar?

_____

_____

_____

_____

_____

_____

_____

_____

_____

_____

Answer your questions.

_____

_____

_____

_____

_____

_____

_____

_____

_____

_____

How was that experience for you? As you do it more, it will get easier and easier. Ideas for questions will flow naturally.

expanding your toolbox

You have the opportunity to be very creative in using your positive history to develop your present and future. Affirmations and your own Inquiry Exercises are wonderful, but why stop there? Is there a creative project that will enliven your inquiry or give another dimension to positive memories you have recovered? Collage is a powerful and accessible medium for expression. The supplies are not expensive and anyone can do it.

Perhaps you will feel motivated to start a daily process for journaling to record and savor the positives of that day. Can you put your own spin on one of the previous end-of-chapter activities? Whether through writing a few paragraphs or singing in the shower, taking a little time each day to focus on the positive causes a powerful shift in your sense of self.

Perhaps sharing this process with your close friends will support you in keeping a positive self-awareness strong in your consciousness. Which people in your life would you like to be able to share the positives with? Is there anyone to whom you would like to say, "Life is so amazing..."?

As you determine who would be open to this process, be conscious about what you share. A few unsupportive words can really sap your enthusiasm. If you're challenged, recall a concept from the beginning of this book: we each must undo the idea that the negative is real and the positive is not to be trusted. Lifting yourself and others up with compassion and care, rather than generic cheerfulness, is basic and ordinary. Politely excuse yourself from conversations that are becoming destructive for you. You might even jot down a few ideas for changing the subject, ending a conversation, or asserting yourself.

Some people hear others' good news and immediately launch into a recitation of their troubles. As you pick up on how people in your world react to sharing the positive, keep in mind that their perspective will likely be different from yours. They may not have questioned the habit of self-minimizing and self-doubting to the degree that you have. People with these tendencies are not bad or weak; their mental habits are the norm in our culture.

No one can take away the positive realities of your self and your history that you've written about. You can share this book or simply make a point of asking at least one question about what's going well in a friend's life each time you speak with her or him. We tend to support each other through talks. We vent to one another—blowing off steam and sharing our worries as well as our hopes. Acknowledging the positive will not prevent you from giving or getting support through venting. Furthermore, repressing sorrow, grief, or anger will not help us. Owning the positive does not turn you into a Pollyanna.

Trust your creativity and your gut instincts as you choose words, phrases, affirmations, and creative projects. Keep whatever degree of privacy you need. Let yourself use words that strike you, even if your husband, best friend, or neighbor might find them odd. This is about creating what you want in life. You have a right to your vision.

references

American Society for Aesthetic Plastic Surgery (ASAPS). 2004. *Cosmetic Surgery National Databank Statistics*. Los Alamitos, CA: ASAPS.

Berg, I. K., and K. Shafer. 2004. Working with mandated substance-abusers: The language of solutions. In *Clinical Work with Substance-Abusing Clients*, edited by Shulamith Lala Ashenberg Straussner. New York: Guilford Press.

Capacchione, Lucia. 2000. *Visioning: Ten Steps to Designing the Life of Your Dreams*. New York: Jeremy P. Tarcher/Putnam.

De Groat, B. 2004. www.bus.umich.edu/Positive

Pennebaker, James. 1997. Writing about emotional experiences as a therapeutic process. *Psychological Science* 8:162-166

Seligman, Martin. 1998. *Learned Optimism: How to Change Your Mind and Your Life*. New York: Free Press.

Carlene DeRoo, Ph.D., is a psychologist with over fifteen years of practice experience specializing in pain management and mind-body connections. She was assistant director of a large metropolitan pain management center and was the director of the Behavioral Medicine Program at a Veterans' Affairs Medical Center. She is a member of the American Psychological Association and is past assistant director of the pain center at Buffalo General Hospital. She earned her doctorate in clinical psychology from the State University of New York at Buffalo and is a diplomate in behavioral medicine.

Carolyn DeRoo is a freelance writer currently promoting writing classes for a community writing center in Oakland, CA.

Carlene DeRoo and Carolyn DeRoo are a mother and daughter writing team. Please visit them at **www.whatsrightwithme.net**.

Some Other New Harbinger Titles

Angry All the Time, Item 3929 $13.95

Handbook of Clinical Psychopharmacology for Therapists, 4th edition, Item 3996 $55.95

Writing For Emotional Balance, Item 3821 $14.95

Surviving Your Borderline Parent, Item 3287 $14.95

When Anger Hurts, 2nd edition, Item 3449 $16.95

Calming Your Anxious Mind, Item 3384 $12.95

Ending the Depression Cycle, Item 3333 $17.95

Your Surviving Spirit, Item 3570 $18.95

Coping with Anxiety, Item 3201 $10.95

The Agoraphobia Workbook, Item 3236 $19.95

Loving the Self-Absorbed, Item 3546 $14.95

Transforming Anger, Item 352X $10.95

Don't Let Your Emotions Run Your Life, Item 3090 $17.95

Why Can't I Ever Be Good Enough, Item 3147 $13.95

Your Depression Map, Item 3007 $19.95

Successful Problem Solving, Item 3023 $17.95

Working with the Self-Absorbed, Item 2922 $14.95

The Procrastination Workbook, Item 2957 $17.95

Coping with Uncertainty, Item 2965 $11.95

The BDD Workbook, Item 2930 $18.95

You, Your Relationship, and Your ADD, Item 299X $17.95

The Stop Walking on Eggshells Workbook, Item 2760 $18.95

Conquer Your Critical Inner Voice, Item 2876 $15.95

The PTSD Workbook, Item 2825 $17.95

Call **toll free, 1-800-748-6273,** or log on to our online bookstore at **www.newharbinger.com** to order. Have your Visa or Mastercard number ready. Or send a check for the titles you want to New Harbinger Publications, Inc., 5674 Shattuck Ave., Oakland, CA 94609. Include $4.50 for the first book and 75¢ for each additional book, to cover shipping and handling. (California residents please include appropriate sales tax.) Allow two to five weeks for delivery.

Prices subject to change without notice.